The Collapse of Liberal Empire

The Collapse of Liberal Empire

Science and Revolution in the Twentieth Century

Paul N. Goldstene

New Haven and London   Yale University Press

1977

Published with assistance from the Louis Stern Memorial Fund.

Designed by John O. C. McCrillis
and set in Baskerville type.
Printed in the United States of America by
The Vail-Ballou Press, Inc., Binghamton, New York.

Published in Great Britain, Europe, Africa, and Asia
(except Japan) by Yale University Press, Ltd., London.
Distributed in Latin America by Kaiman & Polon, Inc.,
New York City; in Australia and New Zealand by Book & Film
Services, Artarmon, N.S.W., Australia; in Japan by
Harper & Row, Publishers, Tokyo Office.

Library of Congress Cataloging in Publication Data
Goldstene, Paul N   1930–
    The collapse of liberal empire.
    Includes bibliographical references and index.
    1. Liberalism—United States. 2. Liberalism.
3. United States—Economic conditions—1971–
I. Title.
JA84.U5G65   1977   320.5'1'0973   76-27367
ISBN 0-300-02029-5

To Patty, James, Claire, and Beth

"The best book is the world."

There's an eagle in me and a mockingbird.

Carl Sandburg

Contents

Acknowledgments

Certain people directly participated in the formation and production of this book. Elizabeth C. Nicholson and Carolyn D. Hopkins grappled with versions of the manuscript which differed only in the details of their unreadability and successfully transformed them into useful drafts. My colleague in the unusual profession of political science, T. Eugene Shoemaker, provided an intellectual sounding board and imparted a very necessary enthusiasm during the working out of a substantial part of the content. As editor, Marian Neal Ash was consistently sensitive to what I was trying to accomplish, and equally consistent in encouraging publication, and my copyeditor, Maureen L. Bushkovitch, offered carefully considered thoughts about clarity and structure that are here incorporated. Mignon S. Gregg, Robert J. Duman, Bernard F. Flynn, Jr., Ted W. Isles, Lucinda S. Jassel, Maria R. Kostello, Robert T. Kostello, John C. Livingston, Jonathan Sharp, Michele J. Shover, and Rick Tilman read the manuscript in its totality or in part and made suggestions that resulted in contributions to the substance or form. At California State University, Sacramento, the University Foundation accorded needed financial support, and the department in which I toil, under the direction of Paul R Murray, provided freedom from many of the political concerns and frustrations which characterize academic existence.

There are others, some directly involved, but fundamentally by indirection, who are profoundly a part of this book. Each knows best what they are being acknowledged for, and I thus feel free to thank them here in generalized form. They are: Lester G. Lewis, Anna G. Lewis, Irving Turner, Nettie L. Turner, Benjamin J. Lawrence, Ann R.

xi

Lawrence, Edith D. Bubar, S. Leonard Cohn, Gilbert M. Frimet, Al Harris, Conrad Joyner, James E. Lyons, Theodore L. Putterman, Lloyd Rodnick, Michael F. Singman, Richard G. Stoll, Harriette Warner, and, of course, those most properly acknowledged in the dedication that precedes.

Introduction

By assumption, attitude, and ideological reflex, Americans are liberals. They are liberals in opposition to democracy, as they are liberals in opposition to conservatism. This is historically true of Americans, however the politically shrewd, and politically ignorant, employment of "conservative," "liberal," and "democratic" vaporizes these terms beyond recognition and content. The despair and lost sense of purpose which currently pervade the American order are not the travails of a democratic polity, but manifestations of a liberal logic unfolding, a liberal nation in reaction to the feudal actualities of a corporate and technological world, and to the democratic demands which these inadvertently produce. They are symptomatic of the conflicts which emanate from an interwoven commitment to material productivity and the primacy of the individual. They represent the inner contradictions of a liberal people turned upon themselves.

Confusing liberalism with democracy, separating politics from economics and technology, Americans fail to come to grips with a reality they cannot and, indeed, refuse to understand. Yet, only by facing the truth of itself will political America begin to discover a rationality which now eludes; to perceive as prelude to reasonable action. To understand the problems of America, the ardent advocates of the "liberal" persuasion, and its equally ardent "detractors," must probe the essential truth of liberalism itself. The failure to do so produces a systemic anguish and confusion, within which the world appears in flux, cut loose from its ideological moorings, where established expectations are scattered by forces beyond control and, indeed, beyond identity, an order wherein no one appears to know what anyone else is talking about.

Here is the crisis of the American system, the crisis of a liberalism which must come to terms with itself if it is to render rational the problems and realities of the age. America must ultimately confront the facts and implications of its own liberalism. What is needed is theory, not "celebration" and ideology.

This book, then, is an attempt to formulate a theory of change which might have empirical application to the United States; any such attempt, to possess explanatory and, possibly, predictive power, must insistently focus upon the phenomenon of power itself. An analysis which emerges from a commitment to change and from the realization that change involves power in all its nuances and ramifications must insist that for change to have a substantive influence on human existence, for change to be real, it must find its premise in the actual stuff of power. A perception of power involves perception of the self and the world, because such perceptions are themselves fundamental elements of power realities. Hence, the liberal view of its own history and purpose is crucial to comprehending power in a now corporate system if the inner reality of its condition is to be understood. In America, this involves a grasp not only of what a liberal America was, but what it has become, in terms of the power configurations which determine its system. It demands an idea of what a postindustrial condition connotes in terms of the substance of power and power relationships, what the technological ingredients of modern power—as opposed to illusions about such power—are, what systemic implications these ingredients contain.

If radical change refers to the enhancement of freedom or, as Hegel would have it, to the advance of ethics in the day-to-day affairs of human beings, a "radicalism" which dismisses liberalism and, hence, what America is, without attempting to penetrate its being and dissect its

illusion from its fact can be of no political use. A theory
of change can devolve only from what exists, certainly not
from a posturing which prefers to condemn reality through
platitudinous response. It will not do to assume that theories
of change suitable for systems struggling for capital accumulation are relevant to a nation which is profoundly postindustrial in its wealth and power arrangements, and which is
precisely characterized by a surplus of capital accumulation
and the internal pressures this fact sets in motion. A
"radical" model for a corporate and liberal America must
be grounded in the power realities of its own political
economy, its own history, and its own essential existence.

Power invariably pervades and controls. Either a liberal
America will perceive the nature of this power, and set it to
its own rational purposes, or it will render all within its system subject to a monolithic domination, and a liberal
civilization will truly end in collapse, instead of asserting
what is not only remotely possible, but finally historically
possible. As Sandburg puts it, in regard to another crisis
which represented what must finally be viewed as a radical
transformation, America is again enmeshed "in the mixed
shame and blame of the immense wrongs of two crashing
civilizations." But now these civilizations are no longer North
and South; they are capitalism and science. Only by first
penetrating the corporate realities of its own power can a
liberal America discover the tremendous political implications of the fact that "there is an ineradicable tendency in
sound technology to go on to purely scientific interest and
breadth of social thought."* Only then can it act on the realization that within the dissolution of the current liberal
despair exists the necessary seedbed of its contemporary
possibility.

I

TRADITION

To every action there is always opposed an equal reaction: or, the mutual actions of two bodies upon each other are always equal, and directed to contrary parts.

Isaac Newton

1. The Ethos of Political Balance

In his attempt to find reality and establish purpose, man seeks a sense of harmony, a sense which accords meaning and limits to existence. Pursuit of the harmonious, conscious or not, is pervasive, dominating serious human concerns. This drive for harmony is crucial within man, informing all actions and thought. Whether inherent or learned, its inner aesthetic is a key motivation of all human behavior even, at times, reaching into the domain of survival itself. As man searches for the rhythms within himself, so he searches for the greater rhythms in the world and the universe. Man orders his existence according to harmony discovered, the absence of total symmetry propelling him forward in quest of that not yet found. Within himself, man seeks stasis; in his art, proportion; in his science, equilibrium; in his mathematics, elegance; in his thought, symmetry; in his politics, balance.

All political ideas are utopian because, in an ultimate sense, all political ideas represent an effort to introduce some conception of balance into the relations of man to man. Directed by a doctrinal commitment to a balance which ought to be, all who contend in politics are controlled by some a priori notion of harmony, and all political speculation advances a consequent vision of balance or imbalance in what is. Those who find balance or its absence are seldom aware that they do so, regardless of the sophistication of their argument and position. The assumption of balance is too inherent often to be recognized.

He who finds balance seeks to preserve it; those who discover imbalance strive to transform the present condition. Discontent with what is, since imbalance, once perceived, is intolerable, they urge a return to the balance of a supposed past, or a forward movement to a projected balance ahead.

Thus the dialectic, motivated by the historic absence of a stable balance, guides the social universe to an ultimate condition of balance, wherein all discordant features are exhausted or, depending on the writer, where the search for balance continues, but on a higher and more humane level.

That the common language of political contention replaces "balance" with "good" or "rational" or "just," should not confuse the issue. It is an ultimate conceptual reality that conservatives, reactionaries, and revolutionaries, whatever the interior details of their formulation, presuppose an a priori version of balance which informs their argument and dominates what they propose. Who prevails, in an age of science, ultimately depends upon the facts. But without a conception of balance, there is no audience. Those who would politically persuade are attended to only to the extent that—and only for so long as—they seem to offer a particle of the greater harmony that is the perennial object of human search.

There are, of course, at any historical moment, a plethora of conceptions about the balance that exists, and about that which should. For some, the balanced order is a consequence of equality; for others, only disharmony and turmoil can result from such a departure from the natural ordering of human qualities. These are the essential starting points; the particulars, myriad in detail, form, and complexity, follow. Yet, despite the variegated ingenuity of the human mind, every operative political system is dominated by one certain version of economic, social, and political balance. This establishes the conceptions and vocabulary of the order, articulating them through a prevailing ideology that motivates action and camouflages the realities of power. It creates the *Volksgeist* of the population; the *Weltanschauung* of the person; that view of the world which controls perceptions of what is, and limits the possibilities of what might be. It is agreement about the political balance which transforms an aggregation of human beings into a political "system." Indeed, agreement is the system.

2. The Nature of Liberal Man

The version of symmetry which holds, and always has held, Americans together is that of liberalism, a notion of balance that begins, according to the conventional wisdom of its spokesmen, with the political formulations of John Locke. Since early in the history of its English colonization, America exists under and within "the tyrannical force of Lockian sentiment."[1] This is truly a tyranny of the mind, carrying with it an explicit and particular assurance of political symmetry, as it exists in supposed fact, and as it should exist in ideal conception. The doctrine, theory, and ideology of liberalism become an expectation, deeply conditioned into the intelligence and reflexes of those who form the American nation. Assaulted by aristocratic vestiges of feudalism on one front, and the democratic forces of socialism on the other, liberalism is long a major factor in the politics of Europe. But it never flourishes within its European seed ground as in America where, essentially free of its war with aristocracy, it forestalls the incessant demands of democracy through the enormity of its economic yield. For three centuries, no country is as liberal as America.

The liberal idea of balance is grounded in a particular version of the human personality. This is a view of fundamental importance, so deeply engrained that only with difficulty can most people within its reach think beyond the limits of its axiomatic truth. Yet, such largely unconscious agreement about man is the direct antecedent of the balance which forms the adhesive of the order.

With one exception of historic significance, all the great projections of what man has the capacity to become visualize an ultimate equilibrium wherein man comes to terms with himself and the world; where the inner personality is no longer in conflict with itself and finds harmonious relationship to the outer world. The one exception is liberalism. Any vision of human perfectibility, whether the elitist perfection of Plato's Republic, or the egalitarian perfections of Jefferson and Marx, eludes the liberal mentality because it violates its sense of what is real.

Not that the liberal cannot conceive of perfection; his notion of it is very clear. In a universe governed by the rational dictates of natural law, he who attains perfection is a totally rational being who, through the application of his properly nurtured inner reason, discerns the entirety of the laws of nature. As a result, he comprehends all there is to comprehend about reason, truth, and morality because, within the Rationalist foundation of liberal thought, these are assumed to be inherently a part of each other. A perfection of understanding implies a perfection of behavior. One who is totally reasonable must, by definition, act according to the dictates of reason itself and, if every particle of mankind attains complete rationality, a universal perfection will prevail. All will agree, disputes will end, and the need for politics will dissolve in a world attended by the harmony of rational accord.

Defining perfection, the liberal denies its possibility. Unlike the democrat, he cannot even entertain it as a projection. By categorical assumption, the liberal knows that man is not perfectable, that reason and emotion are dual within his nature, locked in perennial struggle for supremacy over his actions. It becomes the abiding liberal fear that the passions and appetites of man will overwhelm what is rational within him, and that, among the passions, what Adams depicts as "the *passion for distinction*"[2] is the most pervasive, expressing itself in myriad behavioral forms.

What makes the great liberal writers unusual—and, perhaps, unique—is that they include themselves in their own assumptions. Reason within any human being, no matter how superior the capacity, can never be educated, trained, socialized, or otherwise nurtured into the perfection of the fully rational man. To allow this would require the dissection of the personality into its constituent parts, permitting the emotional to be discarded and the rational retained. Such a feat is impossible because it involves artificially dividing that which in nature is one; and, importantly, what is impossible for all is not possible for some. Despite his certainty that a few exist whose inherent capacity for reason is vastly greater than that of the many, the liberal is equally certain that even these few—the potential members of the political elite—are subject to the subversive influence of the interior passions and to the distortion of the reason which must result.

Such a view of man has enormous political consequences. Almost all forms of rule are categorically unacceptable. There is no philosopher king; there can be no Burkean elite; a rational majority is a figment of democratic delusion. The foundations of conservatism and democracy, the insistent opponents of liberal domination in America, are thus rendered impossible by liberal assumptions. All forms of the state are subject to the appetites of those in office, and such rule of the emotions, whether that of the one, the few, or the many, is ultimately and equally tyrannical. Each is equally destructive of the rule of right reason and, in the final analysis, it is right reason which must prevail.

The idea of a rational natural law is ancient, its origins arcane, and lost in the intellectual recesses of the Western tradition. But the notion of the individual, with personality, with reason, with morality, and with rights, a creature not of community but of natural law, who exists prior to all social convention, is a Rationalist invention. Within liberalism, the major political articulation of the Rationalist conception, the central stress is on rights, around which all other aspects of personality revolve. Only the exercise of rights permits the search for the reasonable beyond man as well as for the reasonable within; the historic application of human reason in the quest for the true and the good in the universe, each inherent in the greater rational order of which they are part. It is the operational reality of rights that allows this quest, and it is the equal possession of rights that renders men equally a part of the political sovereign, the foundation of the conception of popular sovereignty and, consequently, legally equal as citizens.

The importance of rights in the liberal version of Rationalism is enormous. That rights are natural to man, and their exercise the vehicle of the developing application of reason to the physical and social universe, is as old as the liberal tradition itself. Since, in a state of nature, rights are vague and unenforced, government is required for their definition and protection, for the translation of natural rights into civil rights. But, if the state is necessary to improve and guarantee the natural liberty of man—if the dual contract of Locke is enunciated for this purpose—the passions of those who rule render the state the greatest danger to liberty. If an elite of the most reasonable shall rule, and if the many are rational enough to agree, this elite cannot be trusted, even while it cannot be done without.

What the liberal thus proposes is a dilemma, a dilemma which derives from the political verities and controls the entirety of his political position, a dilemma resolved only by appeal to a conception beyond political man. Reason is the goal, rights the expression and mechanism of its attainment, and passion, manifested in power and tyranny, the historic obstacle to the progress of rational discovery and application. Men strive for reason, but are controlled by appetite. If social harmony is to be achieved, it will not be a harmony of human perfection; it is not the nature of man, not even the nature of elite man, which will bring it into existence, but a system established precisely to countervail the inherent tendencies of mankind.

All predilections about the nature of man eventuate in considerations of power. To recoil with disgust and aversion to the very thought of power is an affectation found in those who, perceiving themselves the most "liberal" of liberals, are not liberals at all. Far from denying the existence of power, the whole of the liberal tradition is dominated by a fear of it, a fear grounded in an understanding that power is necessary to the realization of the rights it threatens to destroy.

This fear preoccupies every element of liberal thought, controlling its analysis and prescription. That liberals despise power, that they labor incessantly and ingeniously to nullify and even eliminate the power they would establish, only reveals its central place in the universe of their thought. The civil wars within the liberal movement are often ferocious. But the thread of liberal continuity, what holds liberalism together as a movement, is a profound fear of necessary power, a fear that flows from a certain knowledge that power must be wielded by men, and that while men strive to develop and employ the reason within themselves, even the most rational are likely victims of the passions, the far side of the self which perennially lurks, awaiting the opportunity to sabotage the workings of the reason. Liberalism, in its essential thrust and disposition, becomes an attempt to concurrently establish power and control it, by placing ultimate confidence, not in man, not in any person, not in any group, but in what is best understood as a liberal power system.

It is the enormous stress on natural rights which forms the language of the liberal tradition and instructs its reputation. But it is not this that produces its political consistency. Liberal deviation from its supposed commitment to rights is well noted, especially by its historic opposition. This is because the real liberal concern is not rights, but that which, in the ultimate political perspective of liberalism, is the only guarantee of the reality of rights—the rational arrangement of power. It is this which finally controls the liberal view of man, of society, and of economics. In fundamental disagreement with the democrat, who pays lip service to natural law while resting his case in a majority of the sovereign people, the liberal pays lip service to the sovereign people, and the state which they presumably establish, but finds his real position in those dictates of the natural law that reveal the inner necessity of balance.

Thus, the liberal advocates the advancement of reason by placing the improvement and protection of rights in the hands of a state which comprises the greatest danger to rights and, hence, to reason itself. In this formulation of its fundamental dilemma, the symmetrical impulse of liberal thought is revealed. It permeates its political result, directed at bringing power into accord with laws of nature that cannot allow power to exist except in symmetrical proportion. In coming to grips with the dimension of power, the liberal renders his central purpose—and his controlling aesthetic—understandable.

Liberalism, according to the accepted version, is traceable to Locke. But it flows, in fact, from an earlier formulation. In its implicit political idea, liberalism is less the child of Locke than of Newton. It is the third law of the physical universe which provides the crucial inspiration to the men of the seventeenth century seeking a new foundation for the civil order. All things in motion are in opposition. Particle counterposed to particle, action and reaction among elements equal and opposite, the brilliance of the conception residing in its universal application, and finding its political translation in power counterposed to power in the proper ordering of the great human realms of economics, society, and politics.

Although notions of action and reaction possess a shadowy existence in previous exposition and suggestion, in the work of Hobbes, Galileo, and before, it is only with Newton that the idea of power balanced by power arrives as a sophisticated conception, capable of providing the foundation for a rational political order. This is a revolution, not because it explains particular events, but because the same set of formulations can now claim to explain everything; all realms of human concern are subject to the same laws, the natural laws which control the universe, the earth, and man.[3] It is out of the Newtonian revolution that liberalism emerges.

Within this conception, elegant in its deceptive simplicity, liberal thought discovers its rationale, its morality, its system. The omnipresent thrust of the liberal tradition is an attempt to replicate the physical universe, as expressed through the laws of Newton, in the constitutions of man, an effort which may render more rational the relations between man and man. In social existence, and within the inherent personality of man himself, the elements of man's inner duality, reason and emotion, contend for supremacy. The passion within each contains a tyrannical disposition that can only be controlled by the existence of the identical disposition in another. Because man cannot divest himself of his own nature, and the perfection of his reason is beyond reach, tyranny is averted only when the greater orders of economics, society, and politics are organized to divert the tendencies of human nature into a larger Newtonian balance, a balance which not only serves reason, but is social reason itself. If power is the *bête noire* of liberalism, balance becomes the *raison d'être* of its order. Reason must prevail, and what reason dictates is balance.

Since power cannot be denied without the a priori denial of human existence, it must be cancelled by the introduction of even more power into the system. Despite the disrepute of faction in the announced liberal position, a factional politics is crucial to its success. Faction must oppose faction, yielding an order wherein the natural disposition toward tyranny is frustrated by an equal gravitational pull in the opposite direction, where the elements which comprise the system are perennially in motion while the system remains the same. What the liberal traditionally seeks in the realm of power is the factional tension of a dynamic equilibrium.

The problem of power is thus not resolved through an impossible personal reformation, but is a matter of its ordering. This is true because all power is political; economic and social power is ultimately translated into political power as it becomes employed in the pursuit of public influence and effect. The only rational order is plural, where loci are counterposed to loci in an inexact duplication of the natural laws of the universe which Newton so brilliantly describes. If the system works, the result replicates the natural tension of dynamic balance. All of this is so axiomatic to the liberal mind that it becomes less conscious formulation than reflexive assumption. But to understand it is to grasp the essential foundation of the liberal tradition, the nuances, variations, and innovations which are its historic derivations, and the basis of its turmoil in the present world.

The ideology of liberalism presses for an atomization of power, a factional politics which sets loci against loci in the search for a Newtonian balance of forces in motion. Beyond this, it strives for a bifurcation of conception reflected in the difference between power and authority, between the man and the office, crucial distinctions in the liberal political universe. The proper response to authority is loyalty; that to power, resistance and revolution. Any act of the state must be grounded in authority—legal power as distinct from power itself—if the act is properly one of the state. Actions based on power are only of man and command no loyalty, and a state that habitually predicates itself on power reaches a point where the contract is abrogated, consent is dissolved, authority is withdrawn into the sovereign, and the state no longer exists, because a state without authority is a liberal impossibility. That which defines authority is invariably a matter of compliance with the social fictions that dominate an order and, in the liberal order, these fictions are constitutional.

Within such a system a final arbiter of the contract is required and clearly this should be composed of the most rational of the rational. Thus the state is ultimately controlled by a political sovereign which, in the final analysis, can dissolve it, upon the pronouncement of such a necessity by the proper elite. But the traditional problem of who guards the guardians, implicitly recognized by Locke, is never resolved within his own formulations. In Europe, the battles are elsewhere. To replace the absolutism of dynasty with the absolutism of reason is enough. Among European liberals, conditioned to an authoritarian tradition, the major focus is on constitutional limitation, not on control of those who rule under a constitution, not on the importance of faction, although Montesquieu makes an important contribution to this subsequent preoccupation of liberalism. Still, a philosophy which assumes that none, no matter how elite, can be trusted, and then elevates an elite to a position of final constitutional control, poses a logical and factual dilemma. It is the American liberals, free of the pressures of dynasty and, perhaps as a result, of the illusion that once absolute authority is dissolved the constitutional state can be trusted, who make the historic effort to come to grips with the problem of how a government composed of human beings subject to the inherent passions of their own personalities can exist, and yet be controlled.

Political philosophy finds its tangible results in the attitudes of human beings; it is this which ultimately determines its significance or insignificance. A doctrine or theory that does not infuse the attitudes and values of a people, that does not become a part or the entirety of its ideology and world view, expresses no relationship to political reality and the empirical actualities of a political system. The way people perceive conditions and the way they respond to these perceptions possesses a deep connection to philosophical abstractions about what the political system is and what it ought to be, and such speculations finally discover their foundations in the articulations of scientific discovery.

Beneath the language of constitutionality in America, what ultimately legitimizes power, and transforms it into authority, is the Newtonian conception of balance, where the proper arrangements of action and reaction eventuate in power in symmetrical arrangement and proportion. Thus is the authority of the state counterposed to, and limited by, an overarching constitutional covenant which delineates and controls it. Thus is the will of the people, whose sovereign expression the constitution represents, set against that of an elite, possessed of superior reason—and, hence, understanding—in matters of natural law and the constitution itself. Thus does the press possess the cardinal charge of casting light into the insidious recesses of the state. Thus do personality and rights contend against the state and authority, because where rights exist authority has no place. Thus are those in public office arrayed against the qualified voters, controlled by the republican principle of periodic election for a specified term of years. Thus is a selective majority to work its political will, countervailed by the constitutional pronouncements of qualified elites who, in turn, contend among themselves for supremacy in any discrete instance. Thus does the need for countervailance, flowing from the assumed realities of the nature of man, yield the liberal construction of the contract society.

All of this is familiar to those who understand the United

States Constitution which, in its own terms, is a work of liberal genius. The scope and intensity of government is controlled by the ideology of the Constitution itself, as well as by its expressed stipulations, and the fundamental liberal distinction between power and authority. Elites compete even as they rule in the name of the sovereign people. Faction rivals faction for control of the several departments of the national locus, wherein nearly all who hold public office are restrained by a complex series of refining elites, the few free of this controlled by an electorate of the substantially propertied. Extrapolating from Aristotle, and then from Montesquieu, the rule of the many resides in the House of Representatives and, because the potential tyranny of this, beyond all other tyrannies, must be opposed, the rule of the few characterizes the Senate and the judiciary, while the rule of the one becomes expressed in the executive department. What results is a projected balance of democracy, aristocracy, and monarchy, dissipated into functional categories, with aristocracy favored to the extent that liberals can accord such emotion to any governmental form.

Beyond this, in accord with the liberal fear of Adams that the mixed constitution will actually produce four concurrent tyrannies, each department is delegated a piece of the functional authority of the others—each house of the general legislature conceived as a separate department—enhancing the struggle of elite against elite and, perhaps, an ability to check the tendency towards tyranny which is likely to appear within any department and work to destroy the carefully contrived balance of the national system. This complex elaboration of force and function within the general government is duplicated in the provisions of state constitutions. And all of it exists against a background of that which is viewed as the greatest political check of all, the national system counterposed to, and in competition

with, a state system, the governments therein controlled by
the stipulations of their internal constitutions, each following the pattern of limited authority expressly delegated
into four separated departments, each possessing an element of the authority of the others and, hence, a checking
ability to be employed against any manifest emergence of
the always-lurking tyrannical disposition. In its perception
of man, its abhorrence of power, and its prescription of a
Newtonian balance, the liberal idea saturates the structure
and function of the American constitutional order. If those
of great property are rewarded at the expense of those of
less and no property, this accords with a natural law that
dictates a correspondence between superior rationality and
wealth, insisting that the preferred position of "the Aristocracy of Wealth and Talents"[4] is only a further expression of reason itself.

That the liberal argument for the balance of constitutional supremacy is later subverted by the conservative institu-
tion of judicial review must not camouflage the intention.
It is not surprising that a people whose distrust of power
translates into a distrust of politicians accords authority
that actually supersedes the Constitution into an institu-
tion which is "above politics," transforming constitutional
supremacy into judicial supremacy. Still, the ethos, if not
the reality, of the contract remains strong in America, its
stipulations fundamental to its operative political system.
The United States Constitution continues as a brilliant
monument to the liberal distrust of power, in any hands
and in whatever form; to the notion that loyalty is never
owed to power, but only to authority; and to the insistence
that once the balance is attained any change is likely to
represent an oppressive distortion. This distrust of power is
informed by the proposition of Plato that, given the nature
of man, other than that of the philosopher king, a good
state, one that rules in the interests of all, will, regardless of

its form, soon degenerate into a tyranny that rules in the interests of itself. But the Platonic solution, the philosopher king and the consequent Republic, is no solution for a position that can trust no one.

The liberal solution owes much to the argument of Aristotle, and then Montesquieu, that only through the proper combination of the three good forms of rule by the one, the few, and the many—the monarchy, the aristocracy, and the democracy—with authority separated into branches, as Montesquieu would have it, can liberty be protected. Divided into two great systems, with all loci of authority set against each other, as the English liberals in North America would have it, this is the only formulation which allows government and the absence of the tyrannies of dictatorship, oligarchy, or mobocracy to exist concurrently. "The accumulation of all powers, legislative, executive, and judiciary, in the same hands, whether of one, a few, or many, and whether hereditary, self-appointed, or elective, may justly be pronounced the very definition of tyranny."[5] With Madison, liberals long accept a loss of efficiency as the price of liberty protected and improved by the state and simultaneously guarded from the tyrannical designs of the human beings who are its actualization.

That men in authority will confound their own good with the general good, that they will discover their own rule indispensable to the well-being of the commonwealth, are historic truths well established in the minds of those who promulgate the American Constitution. Despite a persistent rhetoric which stresses the "good" state and enlightened government, what is good is what is balanced, what is enlightened is what is in equilibrium. Controlled by a strange elitism which will not allow the elite to be trusted, the liberal is finally an anarchist who confronts the state as an unfortunate necessity.

It is the persuasive genius of balance, and the politics of

status quo inherent within the concept of balance itself, which insists that between the "liberty" and "tranquility" promised in the Preamble, the ultimate liberal weight is upon tranquility as a preferred condition. Certainly, "delay and deliberate confusion in government become intolerable in communities where men have decisive social programs that they want to execute."[6] But a fear of efficiency permeates the entirety of the Constitution, reflecting a concern that haste shall not overwhelm balance, a concern which dominates the history of the liberal movement in America. Use of such phrases as "balance of power," "checks and balances," "balance of payments" and of "trade," the more subtle expressions of "backlash" and the "pendulum swings of politics," and indeed, the central conception of a mind being in balance, become common to the parlance and mind of liberalism. Its ethos is well expressed by the habit of a liberal electorate in voting against the party of the president in off-year elections and for the party presumably providing the balance of opposition, by shifting perception regarding the desirability of state versus national jurisdictions, of legislative versus executive authority, as it is also expressed in an adversary system of law which separates law from fact, each to be determined by an independent agency of the judicial process.

Constitution writing may be an art form. All political philosophy may be. So be it. If art enhances life, however artificially, if it is a frill necessary to a civilized existence, then let it be done well. The American liberals have done it well. Their Constitution is a liberal masterpiece. In the ferment of ideas which comprise the intellectual age of constitutional formulation, Newtonian mechanics are pervasive, their influence felt in nearly all subsequent inquiry into, and speculation about, politics. The natural tendency towards tyranny inherent in power in motion necessitates power in motion moving with equal velocity in the opposite direction. What results is balance and, if the state is necessary for the protection and improvement of rights, it is balance which ultimately renders such an arrangement possible. Only a system predicated on a sophisticated equilibrium of potentially tyrannical forces, a system grounded in the central insights of Newton, can bring the reality of rights into accord with the liberal view of the nature of man. That the apparatus of "ordered liberty" is complex is a tribute to the inner complexity of fundamental liberal assumptions.

3. The Nature of the Liberal World

The idea of division into realms is not new in Western thought, the distinction between the spiritual and the secular underlying the two-swords doctrine of the medieval period deriving, at least, from the later days of the Roman Empire. But it is only with the emergence of liberalism that realms become competing and central to the entirety of an ideology, and within such an ideology are complexities far greater than those expressed in the American Constitution. The liberal need to pluralize the social universe, to search for particles that might countervail other particles, is too pervasive to be so restrained. Ultimately, three great realms emerge, which together comprise the totality of liberal existence: the realms of politics, economics, and personality, realms held to be distinct in fact as well as conception. While they interact, while one may function to the benefit or the detriment of another, the reality of the gulfs holding them apart remains.

The development of modern psychological theory owes much to the liberal individualism from which it derives. What liberals classically refer to as "the private sphere of the personality" is also a crucial antecedent to the idea of an equality of rights, from which concepts of civil liberties, due process of law, individual expression, and equal justice under law emerge. The emphasis in a liberal society on privacy, not only in law but as a mode of existence, is a paramount consequence of the liberal perception of personality as a distinct realm within a dissected reality.

But it is the social realms of politics and economics—those which together comprise the concern of political economy—that traditionally capture liberal attention and concern. Between them, the economic realm is of far greater importance than the political. So central is economics to

the liberal outlook that, while politics is always viewed as
arrayed against it, the personality is often understood as
subsumed within it. In opposition to the democrat, who
argues that man finds himself through total immersion in
the larger political life of the community, the liberal contends that fulfillment of the person is precisely based on
protection from the intrusion of political demands. But
escape from politics is not enough. That a man is not truly
a man without an independent financial foundation is a
given of the liberal tradition, thoroughly conditioned into
the aggregate self-conception of a liberal people.

Politics and economics, divided in conception, are distinct in liberal reality. Each is governed by a particular set
of natural laws, and what is rendered unique by nature
must be kept unique in the mind and institutions of man.
The sphere of politics is public, permeated by authority,
and the persistent danger of tyranny. Economics is private,
typified by rights and the promise of victory or, depending
on the writer, at least a successful holding action, against
material scarcity. With the great liberal stress on the integrity of the person—or, more accurately, the integrity of
his rights—it is not surprising that economics are illumined
with much kinder light than that cast upon politics.

Deprived of the supporting bulwark of the Roman Church
by the Reformation and the emergence of secular reason,
man confronts the universe alone. The emergence of
the right to property becomes the institutional support for
the alleviation of the human condition. To the liberal mentality, the idea of rational economic man becomes redundant, the pursuit of wealth emerging as the definition of
productive progress and the general good in the continuing
struggle against material scarcity and, ultimately, as the
liberal definition of rationality itself.

It follows that the amassing of personal wealth, however
ostentatious its manifestations, does not unduly disturb a

liberal people. But a concentration of power does. Success in business reveals superior acumen or intelligence or, in classical terminology, reason, and, paradoxically, is accepted as credential to govern, however personally disastrous the effect of moving from a desirable realm to one that is not. Financial accumulation is admired. That it influences politics is dimly understood and vaguely resented: that economic concentration is, in fact, political power is understood by modern liberals hardly at all. It is, however, well understood by classical liberals, who are anxious to ensure the natural separation of economics from political power, the fundamental device of which is to prevent market power, the control of prices, from emerging, because if power does not exist in economics it cannot be transferred to politics. What they seek is a system of factional balance grounded in the competition of entrepreneurs—a balance of neutralized power—and a failure of the balance is precisely what the free market will not allow.

If to socialists and other non-liberals this appears as delusion, the conception of the market as the neutralizer of economic power is, nonetheless, one of the most powerful abstractions of liberal thought, worked deeply and largely unconsciously into the ideology of a liberal people. Power threatens to corrupt the economic world as it does the political. Yet containing it is a far more simple matter. The natural laws of politics demand elaborate and strenuous action, the result of which is the complex apparatus of the constitutional state. But the natural laws of economics dictate that nothing need be done, that, indeed, nothing is exactly and rationally what must be done to bring economic power under effective and productive control.

The true principles of competition, supply and demand, and the predictability of economic man, later augmented by the iron law of wages, Say's law of markets and money, and the theory of marginal utility, ensure that, while what is natural in politics will result in tyrannical power, what is natural in economics will result in an order of balanced liberty. Moreover, neutralizing economic power encourages productive innovation, thereby dissolving the great historical obstacles to economic opportunity as the battle against scarcity is enhanced. The liberal fear of efficiency in the realm of the political finds its conceptual balance in an emphasis on efficiency in the realm of economics. In the world of many buyers and many sellers, wherein the rational dictates of the market freely function, power is naturally controlled. No wonder that the unlikely emergence of monopoly power in any sector of the economy must, according to the classical writers, be immediately removed from the market and taken over by the state. As Galbraith rightly contends, the attraction of the market to classical liberals is as much, or more, its promise to contain power as it is its potential encouragement of productive efficiency in a world subject to the persistent pressure of material scarcity.

Here is the political allure of the capitalist market—entrepreneur played off against entrepreneur, none able to control prices established by the market itself, resulting in a Newtonian balance of economic forces which discourages the development of financial tyranny, and cancels that which does emerge. It does not matter if this is the earlier capitalism of Smith, the capitalism of optimism, according to which production will eventually outstrip scarcity or, following Malthus and Ricardo, the capitalism of despair, where economic victory is impossible because of the reproductive habits of solvent workers and the tendency of manufacturing production to devour arable land. Either way, the economic is the preferable world, perceived to exist in splendid isolation because of an assumed distinction between the economic and the political function, an assumption so deeply accepted that a reflexive preference for the economic over the political is a manifest feature of the liberal order. Thus is the universe of man dissected into the realms of the political and the economic, one opposed to the other, each properly to absent itself from the affairs of the other, according to the great natural principle of laissez-faire.

The liberal system of power is crucially maintained by keeping distinct in political economy that which is distinct in nature, ensuring that none of the realms of human existence intrudes upon the jurisdictional domain of another. What must be especially guarded against is the likely incursion of political power and authority into the sphere of economic enterprise. The customary usage of the term "intervention" to describe such an event, even by its apologetic advocates, reveals how fundamental the assumption of divided and counterposed realms of human activity is to the liberal *Weltanschauung.* It suggests how pervasively liberal Americans are. Whether employed by American "radicals," by embarrassed capitalists, or by those asserting its tyrannical influence as they look to the conventional wisdom in doing battle against it, the concept of "intervention" demonstrates the tyranny of an ideology seldom consciously acknowledged because it is so universally accepted.

The liberal conception of nature, which divides the universe of man into the realms of the personal, the economic, and the political, bifurcates economics itself into the subrealms of production and distribution. Within this lies the analytic foundation of the mid-nineteenth-century desertion of laissez-faire and the beginning of modern liberalism. Usually credited to Keynes, reform liberalism goes back to John Stuart Mill, whose recognition that the expected harmony of the capitalist order is not automatic leads him to contend that its disproportionate effect on wealth distribution can be mitigated—and socialism avoided—by a political adjustment of economic distribution that will leave production alone. To protect capitalism from revolutionary destruction, government must do more than guarantee performance on contracts. If free production—the absolute core of capitalism—is to be preserved, if the balance is to be ensured, the sub-realm of distribution must become subject to "intervention" by the state.

Since the discovery by Mill that the projected symmetry of capitalism is not automatic, liberals have been at war with one another. Those who maintain the classical position become the Social Darwinists, the formulators of a political version of natural selection, for whom the greatest crime is not poverty but any attempt to help the poor, or those otherwise not "fit," still a powerful tradition in America because it emanates from the fundamental roots of liberal ideology. Herein is found the great tautology of Social Darwinism, which contends that since only the fit survive, those who survive must be the fit; and, in an intellectual transformation from the descriptive to the normative, that those who survive should survive, that what is, ought to be. Of course, advocates of "survival of the fittest" hedge their bets, taking from Spencer all but the idea that property ought to be redistributed once a generation—the device, for Spencer, whereby the balance of nature in its forward progression is assured. Indeed, it is this failure to attend to the problem of economic balance which seriously weakens their influence with a liberal population. Still, predicated on a distorted conception of Darwin, who argues that ultimate competition takes place among species, not within them,[1] Social Darwinism remains a vital force, capable of periodic revival, most effective when camouflaged by a propaganda of economic efficiency.

But it is the followers of Mill who are on the ascendancy in the liberal world, carrying with them the essential perception which motivates the economic proposals of reform capitalism: the perception of an order of balanced economic forces and, hence, of economic power, that is not performing as its ardent champions claim it should. This is reflected, as Garry Wills notes, in modern liberal demands for a periodic reshuffling of the cards; a Square Deal, a New Freedom, a New Deal, a Fair Deal, where people are afforded renewed opportunity to develop their individual capabilities as "earners"; an equal footing at the starting line, allowing them to enter the race and demonstrate how unequal they really are.[2] Here is the foundation of Galbraith's contention that the proper function of the liberal state is to encourage and assist the development of countervailing power, to correct the natural tendency of capitalism to lose its inner balance and, most importantly, to avoid the tyranny which must result.

Thus, the historical role of regulated capitalism is an effort to right the equilibrium of an order presumed to achieve it automatically but which, in fact, cannot because the real tendency of competitive capitalism is not a balance among entrepreneurs, but the elimination of competitors. It is not the well-being of the poor—of whom Mill is not overly fond—but the Newtonian balance of the system which is crucially at stake for reform liberalism. Between Spencer and Mill, enormous differences exist. But if Mill will not allow the poor to starve, his reasons approximate the generational rearrangement of property relations that Spencer will later advocate. The issue is balance. What the neoclassicists of the present age conveniently forget about the basis of their position, the devotees of the "welfare" state promote.

Concentration of wealth denies the early capitalist promise of a general balance of income. Yet, far more critically, control over the sources of wealth, which capitalist accumulation implies, denies the entrepreneurial competition that ensures productive innovation and the liberal promise of a factional balance of neutralized power. The debate may boil over the "issues" of "capitalism" or "socialism," "welfare" or "subsidies," "centralization" or "federalism." But as proponents shift from being more "liberal" or less in shifting situations, the real issue for all liberals is invariably that of power and, finally, of balance itself.

That this is the case is vital to the substance of political struggle in the United States. The economic predilections of reform capitalists produce the contorted hybrid of welfare state and warfare government which characterizes every liberal system in the modern world. Yet these do not reflect a liberal public policy because, in terms of programmatic substance, there is no public policy in the liberal order. Programs do not flow from broad public conceptions. They are the achievements of interests narrowly perceived.

According to the logic of the liberal idea, this is as it is supposed to be. There can be no public policy if there is no conception of public interest, and this cannot exist where the population is subsumed by an ideology which denies the very idea of a public; where society is nothing more than the aggregate of individuals comprising it; where a gestalt that could translate the sum total of interests into something greater than itself is not allowed to intellectually exist. There are only persons—or, in its more modern formulation, interests—who, according to the constitutional fictions of articulated liberalism, have freely contracted into the system, each generation presumably reaffirming the original commitment by not rebelling against it. Despite platitudes to the contrary, a factional system cannot permit community. There can be no sense of country. There can be no sense of public. There exist issues and interests, but no public policy.

Among an aggregate of competitors all there can be is what there is, an abiding search for a Newtonian arrangement of power. To the extent there is a "public" policy in the liberal order, the quest for balance is all that it is about. It is this which informs, molds, and finally dictates the seemingly unpredictable policy substance of liberal politics. If liberals appear to lack consistency, it is because their political morality flows, not from considerations of policy substance, not even when rights are involved as, in a liberal context, they always are, but from a deep desire to establish or preserve the balance. However strange the alliance, however uncritical the support accorded those perceived to have little power, however naive liberal perceptions of supposed allies might appear, the tough fiber of liberal "policy" is invariably a pervasive concern with balance itself.

If enterpreneurial pursuit of profit, rents, and interest is the best assurance of such balance, the liberal emerges as a staunch advocate of the free market. In modern terms—and given increased awareness of the cooperative reality of business enterprise—the pursuit of perceived interests by organized groups is urged by those who, no longer devotees of the classical market, follow its impulse and tradition through a commitment to pluralism, the new conventional wisdom of the liberal idea. When repeated often enough, advocation becomes reality—an arcane trick of the intellect which should not be allowed to screen the fact and purpose of the advocation. Pluralism is a normative vision of the rational society; a vision motivated not, as often claimed, by a democratic desire for equality, but by a liberal quest for balance. It is a construction which reveals the absence of a conception of public and, hence, of the public good, in the liberal tradition. Still, beyond the allure of personality and style, what ultimately matters in politics is precisely law—or public policy. It is, therefore, vital to understand that, in the final analysis, liberal "policy" is not determined by its substance, but by the probabilities of its

promoting that Newtonian balance which, consciously or
not, liberalism incessantly seeks.

Power, not policy, dominates the liberal mind, the pursuit of a reasonable balance becoming the essential truth of
politics in a liberal nation. Possessing no notion of public, a
felt need for community manifests itself, not in the idea of
an equality of power, but in the idea of an equality of
opportunity to enjoy the privacy of the fenced-in back-
yard, closed to all but the admitted few, in protected
seclusion from the threat of the greater world. One flees
the loneliness of cities which never were for the more
spacious loneliness of the suburbs. A pervasive denial of
concentrated power insists that economic conditions are
not a result of deliberate policy, but of an invisible hand
that thwarts all efforts at human control. Revelations of a
Watergate debacle create a national trauma, not because
the principals acquired wealth through illegal manipula-
tions, a kind of larcenous success which is admired and
envied—the real crime consisting of being stupid enough to
be caught and forcing to attention truths more comfort-
ably hidden—but because they sought power unwarranted
by the Constitution, an event, when perceived, that sets in
motion the reflexive liberal anxiety about the human disposition towards tyranny. A non-war in Asia is resisted,
and raggedly brought to a supposed halt, not because the
substance of the policy is found wrong, but because the
power of the executive and the military and little-known
"advisors" comes to be overly aggrandized and of question-
able constitutional certainty.

Those who would rule such an order are best off when
most people do not think about politics and the Constitution. But there are times when the effort to keep people
unconscious fails. When this occurs in America, the liberal
ethos which dominates its mind and psyche records itself
in a vast array of symptomatic effects. Issues are not felt

unless they have a direct and, usually, financial effect. The exception—what renders an issue in America truly public—is when power is perceived as breaking loose, whether it is the supposed power of a force from without, or actions not warranted by constitutional understandings within. At such moments, an important segment of those rarely concerned become ardent, if ignorant, constitutionalists. They become liberals or, more precisely, they overtly manifest what they already are.

Only on such occasions does anything resembling community exist in America. Even the accepted pursuit of material gain does not induce community, serving, as it should, to atomize, not unite. Rarely, as Wills would have it, is there a sense of country, a feeling that the conditions of existence are deeply shared with others who are countrymen. For better or worse, such is the yield of the liberal triumph, and beyond an empty rhetoric, each interest pursues its privately conceived goals with no thought about a larger community which, in the liberal formulation, is an empty abstraction. Indeed, community and policy which can make a powerful claim on loyalty introduce the traditional liberal fear of a monolithic authority which will intrude itself upon the integrity of the person. Certainly a system of self-seeking factions producing a harmony of discord is preferred by a people who harbor more than a touch of anarchy because they despise the thought of power.

Thus does liberal ideology structure the order of politics and economics in its persistent attempt to replicate the balance of Newton in a civil society. The central dilemma of a state which is necessary to liberty and yet the greatest danger to it is too monumental to be resolved merely by a constitutionalism which sets authority against authority, elite against elite, and all elites against the sovereign will, however rational its contractual stipulations. More is required. The counterposition of market and state, neither involved in the proper jurisdiction of the other, is fundamental to the liberal solution. Entrepreneur against entrepreneur, production against distribution, a private press against a public government—the totality of the economic realm is that great counterweight to the state necessary to the liberal search for a Newtonian solution in the affairs of men.

II

COLLAPSE

My weariness amazes me.

Bob Dylan

4. The Trauma of Liberal America

Western historians habitually observe, with overtones of nostalgia and despair, that something irretrievable dissolved in the holocaust of 1914, that what since exists is a world epitomized by the suddenly released manifestations of the collapse of reason. When it is remembered that most historians in the West write from a liberal orientation, this is suggestive. What it expresses is a perceived failure of liberal domination, an order of human control long identified with reason itself. Throughout the twentieth century, this failure becomes increasingly manifest, first in Europe and now in the ultimate citadel of its operational power, the United States. The turmoil of modern politics represents the unravelling of liberal suzerainty, a circumstance of historic proportions, reflecting fundamental disturbances always corollary to a growing resistence to the established order; a vociferous chorus that the basics must be changed, that a new foundation is required. At the center is a crisis of liberal balance, a conception traditional and unquestioned in America until the reality of its dissolution comes to be felt through the full force of events.

Technology, the product and central economic value of capitalism in its struggle with a scarcity which flows from the assumed tendencies of population and human insatiability, is enormously successful. Indeed, its assault on material want has come too close to proving that demand need not be always, that human beings can be free from financial concerns, that man *qua* man might emerge from the outmoded shell of classical economic man, that the aesthetic man of Marx might replace the animal man of history, a creature who, in truth, never was man.

The liberal applauds his achievement, and freezes with terror at the fact that he has freed those never meant to be free. Now unshackled from the endless struggle against poverty—a struggle which Ricardo assured his capitalist colleagues could never be won—the mob is loose. The barbarians are at the gates, pouring through the ramparts of civilization deserted by liberal guardians deluded by democratic pretensions of the universality of human reason. Loosed by the forces of liberal technology, the unfortunate effects of the trade-union movement, and an immigration policy left too long open, the masses roam the civil order, gross in behavior and prejudice, forming silent majorities, power blocs of ignorance, and the characteristic impulses of "middle America."

This is not the common man whose century Henry Wallace declared this to be. It is not the man of the rational majority, that democratic paragon of the Age of Reason. What this man represents, in predilection and reflex, is populism and, finally, a middle-class fascism. With the release of the hordes of the mediocre, the balance becomes shaken and precarious, susceptible to the destructive influence of any charlatan who captures the fancy of a multitude freed by technological abundance from the inner restraints of liberal conditioning.

It is a certainty of Madison that among the potential tyrannies of the one, the few, and the many, the many is the most dangerous, because the tyrants are so abundant and their consequent effects so total. With this, all liberals reflexively agree. Such men must be controlled. But the affluence which catapults them into history cannot be reversed. And now, super bowls, celebrities, and bread and circuses are all that remain to liberal control. Retreating into his fundamental elitism, the liberal reaffirms his certainty that the delicate balance of the Newtonian order must be safely removed from the inferior capacity of the average man.

In the instant of perceived crisis, the liberal views the

release of human beings as the shattering of the balance. Whether it is actually man who has arrived becomes a settled matter. The liberal is certain that man has arrived, and that a manifest lack of reason constitutes his central trait. If the Marxist critique appeals to some, the formulations of Ortega y Gasset fascinate more, and within the dimension of its inherent elitism liberal leadership seeks its answer. It is in Ortega that the liberal mind finds comfort and its central clue, a clue traceable to Locke and Madison and Sumner, and the opposition to democracy that saturates the entire liberal tradition.

That most Americans, despite the egalitarian accusations hurled against them, are also immersed in the liberal ethos of an equality of rights but not of reason, are also deeply protective of the basic liberal right to translate an inherent superiority of reason into a financially rewarded ability, that they too seek the elitism and balance which is the core of the liberal promise, does not occur to those who currently pronounce upon the liberal position. The focus of the liberal is on differences of religion, occupation, region, and ethnic origin and derivation. Where the analysis fails is in its inability to perceive that these distinctions, in America, are subsumed within liberalism itself, that Americans "become citizens by ideology,"[1] that this is what congeals an otherwise diverse population. In America, there are few revolutionaries; there are only those who demand entry into a system that has excluded them. But the dominant liberal perception of the many, however wrong, is of paramount importance. The possibility that the multitudes are themselves inherently liberal is dismissed.

With alarming suddenness, a society in searing contradiction with itself searches for the basis of its discontent. To the liberal mind, the principles of reason which once controlled the world, or at least the world that matters, are under assault, collapsing on many fronts. An apparently

insoluble racism pollutes and divides the order, symptomatic of, and fanned by, the winds of an unemployment that
becomes inherent and structural. The greatest liberal nation
in the world is sickened by a revealed vision of its own imperialism, finding it a repellent but logical part of the expansion of financial investment upon which the system is
built. A huge military and foreign aid apparatus—recently
discovered—is viewed as the aggressive force by those unable to admit its origins as a tool of liberal extension
beyond national borders, and as a pump-priming mechanism in the economy. The exploding power of the state
suddenly seems a frightening visage, and executive ambition
is blamed, with little thought accorded the inflation of
power inherent in an imperial posture in the greater world.
Worst of all, there emerges the rejection of the order by
the best of its children who, unable to face a future as organizational ciphers in the bureaucratic machine, would
follow the tambourine man of Dylan or, in more heavy-
handed style, would howl with Ginsberg, rather than become absorbed into the life-style of commercial hypocrisy
which has replaced the integrity of the person they were
reared to admire.

"The centre cannot hold. . . ." The balance flies apart. All
that was and so recently appeared fixed scatters in atom-
izing motion. A yearning to comprehend yields only the
anguish of frustration as people search out the old, to find
no comfort, or the faddish, to find no result. What is not
understood is that which concurrently controls perception
even while it produces a compelling sense that all is not
right with America. Everywhere power is felt. Suddenly
there are no restraints, no limits, no constitution.

The sense that reason falls apart, that tyrannical power
rushes unchecked into a newly created vacuum, is rooted
in traditional liberal notions about the proper balance of

social forces. When and if large segments of the population begin to suspect that the expected balance has disappeared, that, indeed, the hallowed harmony may never have existed, that they may have been systematically lied to by the expounders of the faith, the consequence must be a traumatic episode in the national history. Cynicism leads to despair, and despair is the precondition for revolution. This state of affairs in America, however labelled, is a crisis of the liberal world view, a reflection of a developing contradiction between fact and explanation. It is a crisis of the search for balance; a condition where what is expected cannot be reconciled with what is perceived.

When the traditional balance, whatever its constituent parts of illusion and reality, no longer appears assured, when conditioning to its expectation is rendered weak and difficult, any ideology which predicates its claim on such balance is in profound difficulty. If that ideology dominates, the totality of the system is jeopardized, assertions of legitimacy becoming increasingly uncertain as they are pressured by an unrequited quest for balance and the order it is presumed to yield. People conditioned to the liberal idea—whether they grasp the fact of their conditioning or not—are trapped by expectations of a world that seems to dissolve as they reach for it. They are unable to respond to their inner need for a sense of harmony, a need which is deeply frustrated for reasons they cannot understand.

Here is the core of the current turmoil that besets a liberal America. What it implies is the failure of modern liberals to understand power which, in proper arrangement, is the necessary precondition of the particular balance that a liberal people seek and which is what their political self-conception is predicated upon. It reflects the fact that because contemporary liberal spokesmen mistake effect for cause, in ignorance of the foundations of their own tradition, they fail to consciously understand that balance is not the consequence of an elite, but is power checked and controlled. A liberal nation must confront the demand for a new understanding of the surging and suddenly unknown elements of power.

The process of action and reaction which produces a balance between the public world of the political and the private world of the economic, is of enormous ideological consequence to the liberal system of power, and it is in these terms that the current condition of America and the entirety of the modern Western world must be understood. New perceptions are at the core of liberal disarray, enfeebling its advocates, dilluting its disciples' ability to recover that confidence which accompanies assured domination. Central among these is the suspicion that in the market civilization there is no market. The free market—vital to the fictions attending the liberal tradition—was, as C. Wright Mills points out, never real in America, except in the agrarian West, and there only for a short time.[2] But what was never real could exist in the mind as long as everyday economic conditions could be construed to suggest that what was not yet the case could become so. The entrepreneur was not so removed from those he employed that his station could not be aspired to, and even the burgeoning corporations retained the human smell and idiosyncrasies of their founders. But now pretense dissolves, and what has long been true intrudes upon consciousness. The crisis of liberalism is an expression of change, but what is changing at a socially traumatic rate is less the facts—although they, too, change—than the widely shared perceptions of the facts. The consequences of a liberal population awakening are fundamental and overwhelming. On the fringes of the ideology, anarchy appears as escape. Conservatism, always ready to employ enormous and uncontrolled power, emerges. The forces of liberalism seem in retreat.

Out of the confusion appears an America increasingly

manifest in its corporateness, its power unbridled and patently beyond economics in its social and political impact, in its technological intrusion into the private realm of the person. The balance evaporates, and a people conditioned to its promise are absorbed by an insidious power they have no means to check, except in terms of a world now past. A people with no conception of public are suddenly confronted by a concentrated power which, in magnitude and effect, is monumentally public.

Still, the elitist reflex, which long comforts the liberal mind under pressure by directing its disdain and antipathy to the "masses," has profound consequences. It drains the energy of analysis, producing a startling ignorance among liberal intellectuals as to the nature of corporate America, allowing their perceptions of power to fall into a profound condition of myopia and confusion. As the corporate order extends far beyond "big business" and begins to characterize the entirety of American existence, transforming people and the world into entities new and strange, those who affirm the liberal creed continue to seek the old balance in the old places, substituting fancy for fact as they wend the path of reassurance to political bankruptcy.

Yet a vague discomfort insinuates itself upon liberal ranks. Slowly it dawns that the difficulties which plague the order cannot be dissolved through customary techniques intended to manipulate "mass" mood and behavior; that what they symptomatize is an infection deep within the system, and that what they initially require is recollection of the traditional liberal conception of power moving, at an ever increasing rate, out of balance and, consequently, out of control. Deep within a liberal people, the long dormant understanding that an absence of balance is tyranny begins a difficult struggle towards articulation.

It becomes more apparent that it is not the "masses" who have seized power; that, indeed, it is they who are seized by power; that, in desperation and turmoil, many turn to the comforting slogans of a political "right" which bases its claims in the rhetoric of an earlier capitalism. A few, who think themselves willing to break with an evaporated past, are attracted to a strange "left" which denigrates capitalism as its own alienation propels it into the most fundamental capitalist form of the small entrepreneur independently marketing his own production. In the midst of national confusion, those identified as political "liberals" continue to dabble with defunct tradition as the influence of "big business" becomes an increasingly popular topic of discussion. Yet all seems without effect.

To understand the travail of America, it is useful to recall that "ironically, 'liberalism' is a stranger in the land of its greatest realization and fulfillment."[3] Because liberalism is so successful in America, because agreement to its stipulations is so universal and complete, its domination over mind and action is seldom noticed from within. But Americans are liberals, and the variety of political persuasion and conflict epitomizing the system occurs only within the limits of this overwhelming, if unconscious, commitment. Failure to bring their *Weltanschauung* to awareness does not change the fact that it is as liberals that Americans are in crucial and troubled reaction to a historic shift in the relations of power which dominate the nation and intrude themselves upon existence.

An analysis of power in a postindustrial world demands that the focus must be on corporatism as a generic condition of modern life. It is this which contains the essential clue to the present; a corporate power which achieves a dimension, form, and function that the liberal mind, locked in its prison of classical expectations, and loath to admit the existence of a power so pervasive, cannot understand or even perceive. But considerations of modern power without exposure of its multinational corporate essence is camouflage or delusion—a circle-squaring expedition that yields confusion and cynicism while the central balance of the order is demolished.

In the age of the robber barons, when firms expressed the personality and name of the financial or inventive genius who headed them, when moguls, in the tradition of Horatio Alger, fought their way to fame and fortune; the development of the business corporation, while anathema to Progressives, did not occasion anxiety in the liberal mind. The presence and dimensions of corporations were understandable and, hence, rational. Indeed, the large firm was the vehicle of progress, crucial to the promise of liberal productivity in the endless battle with the scarce availability of the goods of the earth. The company appeared, and often was, subject to the vagaries of life—much as a human being, whose personality and rights it was accorded in law. The wealthy could make mistakes, they could stumble and fall. The vagaries of the competitive market could transform success into sudden and traumatic failure, and the individual who failed with it could evince sympathy or scorn precisely because he could be identified and rationally understood. Those who owned such firms were rich and, of course, had power; but it was power on a human scale, power that could be comprehended, power that might violate the tenets of the market but that did not seem fundamentally to threaten the Newtonian balance of the order. Corporate power was perceived as manageable in dimension, scale, and reach.

With the emergence of the modern corporation, everything changes. The personality of the founder becomes lost, a public-relations vestige of archaic tradition, discarded by a technological demand for organized and coordinated knowledge on a scale no one man can achieve. Planning, however unannounced, replaces the spontaneity of the market, the chance of error cancelled out by the precision of cost-accounting, to which all elements of the firm pay due and increasing deference. As the erratic nuances of temperament are absorbed into the certainty of bureaucracy, the business corporation becomes devoid of personality. All seem the same. Structure subverts what once appeared human; the discord of business and technical genius, long repugnant to some, surrenders to the studied calm of specialized competence—to gray men quietly functioning in gray places, one anonymous element smoothly substituted for its easily replaced predecessor, removed with little reward whenever an equally anonymous authority determines it is worn out or has lost utility.

Technological innovation itself becomes organized, and an organized science, striving to be "useful," comes to be ensconced in great universities, which are eager recipients of corporate subsidy and of the largesse of a state anxious to please business organizations that thrive on the marketable findings and manipulative inventions of the "scientific" establishment. A plenitude of lesser places of learning emerges, filling the need of business and government organization for a labor force trained in the technological yield of scientific discovery. Organization, the regularized interaction of human beings, becomes pervasive. The organization man has arrived. So has the organizational world.

This is a world of vertical integration. Producing corporations, increasingly free of financial institutions as they generate sufficient internal capital to underwrite their own ventures, are transformed into lending agencies relative to firms of lesser magnitude. Companies that once supplied raw materials to producers are bought up by those producers and absorbed, much as the communications and transportation networks necessary to their operations are absorbed. Organized labor, the traditional locus of opposing power, becomes a cacophony of "business unions," integrated into the financial planning of the firm, repaying the favor with unstated quietude and growing loyalty, producing a labor force sold out short and cheaply by a leadership committed to a corporate patriotism, and corporate profitability, planning, and control.

Price competition—the necessary core of capitalism—is integrated and abolished, at first through the clumsy device of criminal collusion, later through administrated prices made possible by industry-wide agreement on a proper rate of return and techniques of prediction so refined that conspiracy is no longer necessary to precisely know the projected prices of the supposed competition. In such manner are prices managed by technological corporations, not only the prices they charge, but the prices they pay to suppliers of necessary elements of production, even those not yet legally integrated, a phenomenon which enormously surpasses the classical definition of monopoly power. Still, the liberal aversion to monopoly remains strong—the great capitalist writers, having urged a takeover by the state in such an event. Instead of monopoly power—the clear ability to establish industry prices and corrupt the balance of the market—what prevails, with uncharacteristic exceptions, is an oligopolistic form, wherein a few vertically integrated companies control prices in fact, if not in law, and where the actualities of competition are addressed to matters of style and advertising, but never to prices.

As Veblen forecast, the essential competition of the system no longer exists among producers, but between producers and consumers.[4] This is only reasonable in an economy increasingly characterized by a sophisticated technological foundation. It is a requisite of the planning necessary to technological production, and of the enormous financial investment which attends it, that price competition cannot be afforded. Neither can the absence of a predictable buyer for the eventual product; too much is involved to allow the uncertainties of supply and demand. In light of mounting evidence that human desire for material possession is satiable, that economic man is not always classically rational, the assurance of markets becomes critical. The ability to plan is at stake. So is an economic ideology predicated on a permanence of scarcity, an ideology which is clearly endangered when an increase in personal wealth results in fewer children, not more, when, despite an eager willingness to extend credit, the urgency of demand goes down as income goes up. These are frightening facts for liberal economists. They can be rationalized through the theory of diminishing marginal utility, but their impact remains. They become a reality that must be changed. Under conditions of modern technology, the liberal order can no longer tolerate capitalism.

The emergence of advertising as an industry so crucial to the working of the economic system that its influence characterizes existence within it, reflects a pressing necessity to create wants; to artificially induce that which, under capitalism, is automatic and natural; to establish demand not only for specific products and particular brands but, far more importantly, material demand as a prime social value. It is with the saturation of the consumption value through advertising that America becomes, in the fullest sense, what Beard refers to as a "business civilization."[5] Yet, of ultimately greater importance to the maintenance of the liberal order is the emergence of the Keynesian state as a principal buyer of its corporate yield. That this results in enormous military production is only to be expected by those of a logical turn of mind. Political problems attending large governmental expenditures in a nation mentally attuned to a private market are substantially eased when legitimized by slogans of foreign aid and national defense. And, with a symmetry worthy of the liberal mind, warfare production serves other needs of those who produce it. A system of highly profitable cost-plus contracts, replete with charge-offs for the required propaganda, in those rare instances when they are brought to general attention, are easily justified as integral to the national survival. Obsolescence is guaranteed—most often before the product is delivered—in a world dominated by an arms race with a sufficiently hostile foreign power, and demand is thus rendered endless and assured. Finally, there is the most crucial advantage of all, a long-range commitment to purchase, free of the uncertainty of market conditions, stabilizing the corporate planning and organization necessary to innovation in an economy of sophisticated technology. Within an order of planned obsolescence, military production becomes the characteristic form, the model to be admired and emulated.

So successful is the political appeal of the warfare state that its ethos is increasingly pervading in all areas of Keynesian advocation. The government of the United States can no longer build a road, engage in agricultural price supports, venture into space exploration, lend money to subversive students—or do anything else—without basing its enabling legislation on a consideration of the international perils of not doing so. Captured by the logic of warfare economics, the labor movement, and even antiwar liberals, find no adequate technique of providing employment opportunities other than magnifying the federal budget for military procurement and production. Inherent in the act of clearing the field for corporate business, the transformation of America into a garrison society and the militarization of the American outlook proceeds.

Thus, while a liberal nation, absorbed in its factional interests, sees nothing, and while liberal leadership devotes its best energies and talents to the effort, the liberal market is demolished, the historic tension between the economic and the political, between supply and demand, among

entrepreneurs competing within an industry, evaporated
into a state economy, an organic realm where the elements
of politics, economics, and personality are not only part of
all others, but where all is the other. The gestalt not allowed
by liberalism has been achieved. Semantics of "intervention" abound, but the act becomes impossible. What
emerges is an industrial authority of enormous concentration, its segments integrated, its ventures conglomerate and
concentric, those on its payroll, "public" or "private," an
ever-increasing proportion of the population. In its essential
economic qualities, it is a warfare system—a system inherently dangerous but precisely designed to meet the needs
of corporate enterprise and, from that perspective, a most
rational application of Keynesian principles. Buttressed
against its own people by the same advertising techniques
which manipulate consumer demand at home it is, in the
reach of its technological surplus, a global system. For liberals suddenly to be concerned that power is out of balance
is one of the ironies of the human condition from which
the pleasures of historical speculation derive.

In the minds of those whose view of the world is steeped
in deep, if usually unconscious, anxieties about the existence of power, an awareness of the corporate realities of
modern existence induces disturbing considerations. Having
come to suspect that something is wrong, that concentrated
power, not fully perceived and free of the controlling balance, is the locus of the malady, the liberal critique floats
in a sea of frustration, seizing on instances of factual flot-
sam and jetsam as they chance to drift through the screen
of analysis. The process of economic and technological
concentration is penetrated by the law of the declining
rate of profits, one of the few theoretical attempts to
explain the inability of the competitive market to survive
the introduction of machines into production—the fruit of
the capitalist stress on technological innovation and the

enhancement of productivity itself. But this theory is associated with Marx, and the liberal mind automatically rules it out, offering nothing beyond urbane nonsense with which to replace it. Lacking an adequate theory, liberals fail to realize that their critique is random, and the closer they get to the major liberal problem of the twentieth century the more obscure it becomes, its very pervasiveness rendering opaque the precise area of real concern, the location of power and the system of power it represents.

If Marx is anathema to the liberal mind, he lends it comfort by insisting that economic ownership is economic control, that both are economic power, and that the translation of economic power into political power is immediate. But in the early 1930s, a new insight appears, major in its importance for modern liberalism and ultimately insidious in its effects—the insight of Berle and Means that ownership has become divorced from control and, by extension, from economic and political power; that an entity new and strange, the manager, is now in command.[6] By 1940, Burnham can advance a theory of total transformation brought about by a "managerial revolution." The managers have assumed domination, while all liberals but a few gazed intently in the wrong direction, concerned about nonexistent differences between capitalism and socialism, expending their concern about concentrated power on those who still appeared to function as classical entrepreneurs. Disturbing as the finally revealed decline of the entrepreneur is, even more disturbing is the subsequent discovery that those who presently control the business corporations are, as Burnham reveals, replicated in type and impulse in the state itself.[7]

In the 1940s and even the 1950s, the liberal could rationalize an escape from the implications of the Burnham thesis; he could still grasp the available straw, buoyed by the thought that America, after all, was more egalitarian than the radical critique could allow. While the old order of a ruling class, predicated on established ownership of productive property, was closed to those of the wrong families, people of "talent" could now gain entrance into the managerial elite which dominated the new system. Indeed, in the more idealized version of the liberal persuasion, power was seen as more pluralized, flowing to managers of discrete firms, no longer unified by the interlocking tentacles of ownership.

But the discovery of managerialism remained a problem. If power was more diffused, it was also more difficult to identify and hold to account, while the possibility lingered that, beneath a pluralistic facade, managers were becoming a new owning, and concentrated, class. Even more dangerous, to admit domination by the managers was to admit to a new order of monopoly or oligopolistic enterprise, one where big business and the state were becoming inseparable, where the boundaries between them were now so subtle and indistinct that the great balancing gulf may, de facto, have been bridged.

This unsettling muse about a totality of power accounts for the years between the first liberal formulations of the managerial order and their reluctant acceptance by the liberal intellectual establishment, a process still far from complete. While spokesmen for the liberal idea continued to pursue the golden age of the market, as some still do, contending with one another over the relative merits of laissez-faire and regulation, the pressures of technological production brought anonymous managers to increasingly total control in an order where the liberal system of power was dimly perceived to be in the process of dissolution.

John Kenneth Galbraith, who in a deeply liberal America might well be the Madison of his era and, in matters of political and social economy, the most influential phrasemaker and conceptualizer of his time, could try to hold the line against liberal despair. Finally bringing to established attention the fact of oligopolies and the economic power they represent, Galbraith—seemingly assuming managerial control—could contend that the balance of price competition yet exists not, in classical terms, from the same side of the market, but from the opposite side. Sellers, no longer arrayed against sellers because of oligopolistic agreement on prices, find themselves in actual competition with large and unified buyers. The monopoly power of the seller is countervailed by the monopoly power of the buyer; oligopoly is restrained by oligopsony.

The managers of corporate America continue to possess enormous market power, as intolerable for Galbraith as for classical liberals; but the system of countervailing power which characterizes modern systems mitigates it and, consequently, reduces the danger of its translation into uncontested political power. If a market power that is not supposed to exist does exist, it is automatically controlled in a manner that accords with the traditional liberal perception of the market. Only now the political realm is crucially involved, the essential obligation of the state no longer being merely the guarantee of contracts, antitrust laws, and fiscal and monetary regulation, but the encouragement of countervailing power.[8]

While the finally-perceived fact of managerial power is slowly absorbed by a reluctant liberal ideology, the same Galbraith, a little older, far more disturbed by the arrangement and uses of power in the corporate system—and perhaps politically wiser—now contends that, appearances notwithstanding, not even those who supposedly manage concentrated economic power actually do so. The demands of production which dictate the flow of power have become transformed. Managers may think they make decisions, they may act as if they do; but the imperatives of a sophisticated technology, for which the crucial factor is an organized group intelligence, render it mandatory that experts make the important decisions, whatever the subject of their expertise, even that of power and organization itself. To wield power effectively, one must possess knowledge of the productive and distributive process and, in a technological system, the experts are the only ones who do. As the entrepreneur gave way to the manager, so the manager surrenders the actuality of power to groups of specialists within something called the "technostructure."[9]

To the extent that Galbraith is correct, it might appear that Veblen's dream has come to be, that the engineers have wrested power from the businessmen—or, in modern terms, the managers—in a joyous triumph of efficiency and reason.[10] But such joy is of short duration in Galbraith's world. The actualities of decision, operating within and among a complex array of anonymous groups, hidden by the very plurality of expertise which is the hallmark of the technostructure, introduce tremendous difficulties into the liberal search for balance. What emerges is a totally new system of power, camouflaged by the scenario of classical capitalism or managerial domination. It is a system that typifies the supposedly private firm as well as a state supposedly laden with public responsibility, a bureaucratic system with vast influence on lives and events through ultimate control of technological policy and its enormous ramifications. Within it, power is impossible to identify and, consequently, impossible to hold responsible, power of incredible scope lost among the Byzantine configurations of the corporate world.

Discerning the locus of decision becomes even more difficult as the great corporations increasingly cooperate in areas beyond that of price administration, reaching into the crucial realm of technological innovation itself. Rendering matters even more obscure is the functional interchangeability of personnel within and between the giant corporations and the state. The power which emanates from this most unliberal combination is more than technological. It is patently political. A system of great corporate structures, concentric in producing operations and conglomerate in dimension; vertically integrated to control prices of raw materials, labor, transportation, communication, and sales; managing prices through oligopolistic agreement; its profitability so vast it is beyond the reach of the money market; absorbing an ever-increasing proportion of the work force; shaping demand through its advertising adjunct; manipulating policy through its eradication of the great classical distinction between private and public; and dominating the mind of the population through its integration of mass media, forms the ruling order of the modern world. Ubiquitous in effect and seemingly mindless, the power of the order is secreted within a plurality of technostructures, pluralized in themselves, beyond identity, and beyond the balance of liberal control.

This is no longer the world of Locke. It is a world of Kafka, rational, perhaps, in terms of what brought it about, yet not subject to the rationality of liberal understanding. Power so concentrated and screened from perception which it increasingly constructs, reflects a world run amok and absurd, a system that defies balance and reason. Thus does the century move to a condition where the effects of power are pervasive, but where its identity is lost.

The emergence of such a condition, implicit in the rise of the managers to power, inherent in the arrival of the technostructure, represents for liberalism the failure of reason and, within this, the crisis of the liberal persuasion resides. The forces of technology place power not only past reason but past recognition, an implicit but basic necessity of the Newtonian balance. The essential pathos of *The New Industrial State* is its desperate quest for a new locus of power which might regenerate liberal restraint, a countervailing power to replace that which, in adject surrender to the imperatives of technological innovation, is absorbed into the dominant corporate order. That some can argue with effect that those who wield such power can be trusted testifies to the emerging importance of a conservative reliance on the assurance that the proper elite is in control, and that no interference with its rule should be allowed because, by conservative assumption, all who might check the elite are, by definition, less than elite. The increasing cogency of this argument within liberal circles finds its underlying condition in a fatigue that reflects the confusion currently rampant in regard to the issue of power.

Even more than private accumulation, technological innovation and production are central values in American society, and it is these which now subvert the reality of liberal man and the rights attendant to his existence. Liberal man becomes corporate man—technology discarding those it cannot use, transforming those it can into agents of the order who serve in unquestioning obedience a will past their understanding. The tyranny which liberalism is devised to prevent is born of the social myopia of liberal perception, propelled by erudite but arcane economic formulations which insist upon the assumption of scarcity in the midst of potential abundance.

Yet, the conservative formulation remains a hard sell to a liberal people and, in the final analysis, to those articulators of the prevailing ideology who now tamper with its ideas. Distrust of power is deep and fundamental. Power of enormous concentration in purpose and effect, hidden from the controlling force of perception, is power out of balance and devoid of reason. Despite the turmoil that currently attends their political outlook, such power, whatever the intentions of those who wield it, and whatever the alleged wisdom they possess, must be tyrannical to a people saturated in the liberal idea. It is this which produces the anguish and frustration of the modern liberal: a glimpse of power intolerable to those conditioned to liberal expectations.

5. The Impact of Imperial Decline

From the time of early exploration and settlement by newly devised joint-stock companies, the corporation is crucial to the American economic experience. But only recently does it encroach upon the liberal mind as the centrally dominant force which shapes the contours of the system. This emerging perception represents a dramatic shift in the liberal outlook, reflecting the enormous growth of corporate power and its bureaucratic manifestations which, in fact, are the product of a deep liberal commitment to the idea of economic expansion.

In its essential formulation, the Lockian contract is a national conception. Yet expansion is inherent within it. Only citizens impose obligations on a state established to improve and protect natural rights through the delineated authority which characterizes the constitutional order, and only the rights of those party to the contract find their governmental translation in the form of civil rights. In regard to all who are not citizens—and not bound by loyalty to the fundamental agreements of the compact—the liberal state has no responsibilities at all. If, in carrying out its obligations to the rights of the national people, the state intrudes upon, and even destroys, what might be the rights of people existing beyond the purview of the contract, these are not rights which a liberal order can technically recognize. The rights of those within the nation are presumed to exist. Beyond this, the liberal contract does not go. Liberalism, historically inseparable from capitalism, is equally inseparable from the national conceptions from which it emerges.

It follows that the liberal idea of an ordered liberty predicated on a power equilibrium is strictly a national idea. Constitutional limitations are only operative where rights are at issue, and rights conceivably possessed by the inhabitants of foreign systems, not being recognized in the contract, cannot be at issue. Despite the presupposition of laws of nature which are universal, and the unfortunate "excesses" of certain elements within the French Revolution, the liberal claim never applies to the rights of man, but only to the rights of men covered by the fundamental agreements of the contract. Indeed, a more extended conception of rights causes liberals to be nervous, as the reaction of English and American liberals to the French claim reveals.

This unstated denial of rights in those who are foreign, a denial inherent in the interior logic of the contract idea, becomes vital to the liberal conception of international politics. Exclusion is the basis of obligation among people in all societies, cementing the society as a discrete entity. No state recognizes much of an obligation to people beyond its jurisdiction but, in an order where a commitment to the idea of rights forms the central rationale of the system, this induces a sense of guilt and a consequent inner tension that begins to pervade the prevailing political existence. Still, it is precisely this denial that provides the basis for Locke's prescription for the prerogative authority, the unlimited and unchecked authority of the monarch to deal as he thinks he must with other systems under the general category of foreign policy.

Such refined abstractions have tremendous influence on the history of a people saturated in the ideology of liberalism, an ideology that promotes expansion through its reflexive need to categorize and divide. This reflex, when applied to power within the system, is a manifestation of the search for balance. But when it demarcates people covered by the contract from those who are not, it becomes the justification for unlimited authority in the realm of foreign affairs. To preserve the balance at home, liberal exclusiveness insists that in domestic politics authority must be subject to countervailance, while in the international arena it must be free of constraint. The exclusiveness of the liberal contract is the basis of the white man's burden, clearly manifested in the general perception of slaves in the United States. Throughout the history of liberal America, people of other nations, beginning with the Indians indigenous to the continent, are not perceived as possessing rights, certainly not rights worthy of respect by the authority of the state and, despite a propaganda that promulgates an equality of rights, plainly not equal to the rights of those party to the contract.

It is, of course, useful for the formulators of liberal empire to cloak such legalistic considerations in a phraseology the population can digest. Any effective ruler must camouflage his real intentions in the language of the dominant ideology, and those who rule America must converse in terms of rights—at times with cynical disregard for reality, more often in the fullness of their own deeply conditioned liberal response. Thus, the conception of manifest destiny, the liberal rationalization upon which American expansion is long predicated, is eagerly accepted by a population enamored of its promise to bring more people and, in its ultimate extension, the entire world, into full enjoyment of the rights represented by the liberal order. Such enjoyment is clearly less apparent to the recipients of such benevolence than to those who would bestow it. Yet the commitment of the American people to the idea of the expansion of rights renders them amazingly myopic about the economic realities of American foreign policy.

What results is a historic attempt to extend the parameters of the contract. Unlike conservatives, who accept any form of the state that can be reconciled with the tradition of the organic nation, liberals are committed to the spread of constitutional government throughout the world, a position which derives from fundamental liberal axioms about reason, power, and man. In thereby urging the expansion of the contract, the liberal does not really violate the fundamental conceptions of his own thought; those delineated parameters which are necessary to the Newtonian idea in politics are preserved. The legitimate boundaries of the system are simply enlarged. Once established, a new order, greater in scope, but no less characterized by constitutional limits, emerges. Thus does a liberal nationalism ultimately express itself, transforming national liberalism into international liberalism, a system to be epitomized by the factional conflict of power and expressed authority which takes place within.

Devolving from the principle of manifest destiny, the most important articulation of liberal expansion in the American twentieth century is the Wilsonian formula for "making the world safe for democracy" within a global configuration of "national self-determination." What is really at stake, of course, is making the world safe for the profitable investment of the corporate dollar and the expanded organization of liberal capitalism. Pressured by enormous aggregates of venture capital seeking profitable outlets, the conception of Wilson insists that self-determination is applaudable only if things are determined correctly, that is, "democratically"; or, in later language, where there exists an eager "free world" recipient of corporate investment. Still, the fundamental idea of the contract, concurrently exclusive and expansionist, maintains its hold on the perceptions of the American people, who, awakening to the realities of the system at home, continue to be obtuse about their application in the world. A technological system concerned to retain the economic, social, and political domination that, for much of the world, and for more and more of its own people, is its most salient characteristic, finally corrupts its liberal foundation. Increasingly, the pretense of ideological justification cannot be preserved, and its formulations overtly surrender to the pressures of venture capital requiring a world that functions as an appendage of its technological, financial, and bureaucratic necessities.

The gross inequality of income which typifies liberal systems is justified by the capitalist assumptions of perennial scarcity in a world of insatiable economic men, who will immediately produce too many children the instant they attain an income that will marginally allow it. From these assumptions, the incredible emphasis on the work ethic, "invidious comparison," and productivity derive; an ethos which insists that the allure of great wealth and the fear of great poverty are mandatory if human beings are to work harder than their natural inclination would otherwise allow. That a being presumed to be rational, and automatically in pursuit of economic gain, requires the societal motivations of wealth and poverty is an anomaly of liberal economics that, over the centuries, bothers few of its ardent advocates, who are serenely certain of their basic vision of the nature of man.

Logic notwithstanding, scarcity is central to liberal thought, as is the resulting contention that those who contribute most to production must be financially motivated to continue to do so. The successful infiltration of these ideas into the world view of liberal populations is a tremendous ideological safeguard against potential reaction to the fact that the poverty, or marginal existence, of the many coexists with the paraded opulence of the few. Presuming the truth of economic scarcity, the poor and the marginal are as vociferous in their applause of the system as are the rich.

But important as the construct of scarcity is, it is no longer the deciding factor in the political pacification of the population. The productive yield of corporate America is enormous, vastly amplified by a technology characterized by an institutionalized research and development that is financed by the tremendous resources of great firms and, increasingly, the classically disinterested authority of the liberal state. As production soars, so do returns and this, when combined with the profitability of imperial ventures, allows a distribution of greater buying power to the population. Here is the great pacifier of contemporary modern liberalism. Under modern conditions, financial liquidity is so enormous that what remains is more than enough to maintain, and even increase, the gulf between the corporate rich and all others, a gulf vital to the operation of an order immersed in capitalist assumptions and values.

Profits accruing from large-scale investment in research and development are more than augmented by the margins flowing from imperial ventures. Particularly in its initial stages, research and development is actually capitalized by the profitability of an imperialism that is then justified on the basis of the military necessity to protect American rights in the world and, more important, American corporate interests in the imperial areas. Thus, the internal affluence that flows from the application of technological research depends for its financing, directly and indirectly, upon imperial investment, where labor and resources are cheap and controlled, and the general tax dollars of the metropolitan power pay for financial guarantees to investing corporations and the necessary military control. In its nineteenth-century variation, this is accomplished by colonial settlement; in the current era, by direct military involvement at times but, most typically and effectively, through the device of local tyrants in the tradition of indirect rule developed by the British in an age when they dominate much of the world. That the rulers of certain nonindustrial countries, surfeited with dollars from imperial investment and purchase, unwilling and, indeed, unable to distribute them among their own populations if they are to maintain their internal systems, now seek to reinvest in the United States, is fitting tribute to the dollar ethic of an imperialism that respects no boundaries of nations and evidences an internal symmetry of its own.

To the modern corporation, the rate of return flowing from foreign investment is crucial, a fact successfully ignored by many economists who insist that the magnitude of such return in relationship to gross national product is not great. The political point, however, is not proportion to national wealth, but proportion to the internal wealth and consequent power of the investing corporation. Of ultimate significance for the maintenance of the status quo at home is the political and social power of business corporations, a power reflected not so much in the direct use of money in the political and social arenas as in the continuing ability of the system to frustrate fundamental change by placating the population with a certain level of income distribution. That establishment economists learnedly miss the point reveals a liberal conditioning deep within the profession of economics, which, bifurcating the world into the realms of the political and the economic, and taking this bifurcation seriously, proposes rational models in place of the political substance of economic decisions—a species of decision which exists, despite the predilection for believing that it is the true principles of economics which autonomously prevail.

It is the enormous return on imperial investment, allowing the lavish financing of research by the great corporations and an increasingly inseparable state, that permits Americans to brag, however wrongly, that they possess the highest standard of living in the world. The bulk of such research is of a military nature, serving the needs of corporate enterprise for planned obsolescence and an assured market. In a revealing twist of liberal symmetry, it also serves the need for control in those areas of the world used as a conduit for the surplus capital accumulation that characterizes and, if unused, threatens, the continuation of capitalist values within the corporate order. Thus does the liberal state finance the research for production that it then buys and employs in the direct interest of those who produce it. The power of the great corporations becomes cloaked with the authority of the state, a configuration of vast power and wealth, opaque to the liberal mind in the actualities of its tremendous concentration, a concentration which precisely becomes the great unsettling force behind the shattering of the liberal balance. In an irony worthy of the liberal predilection for symmetrical arrangement, what the liberal system of power produces through the logic of its commitment to economic scarcity is what threatens its political *raison d'être* and, in the final analysis, the existence of the liberal position itself.

That, until recently, Americans have eagerly embraced "democratic" justifications for the world position of their government, with no insight at all into the imperial reality they camouflage, is testimony to the insular affluence of many, and the expertise of those who merchandise foreign policy. In a country where advertising skill is rewarded far in excess of what is allotted to inquiry and analysis—a country that thus betrays a reflexive preference for lies over truth—it is not surprising that trained intelligence should gravitate into the ranks of professional manipulation. In the land of the "booster," nothing else should be expected. But the remarkable success of the liberal rationalization of its own foreign policy is based on more than this. It also reflects a lack of resistance in the world serious enough to provoke the thought among liberals that, under Pax Americana, not all are happy with the arrangement.

Now, however, and especially since 1945, resistance throughout the nonindustrial world to a continuation of its role as a dumping ground for the surplus venture capital of corporate enterprise emerges, a resistance reaching a magnitude that renders it the most profound political fact of the twentieth century. Within the liberal order, the suspicion grows that the people of the nonindustrial nations really are people, that they may be entitled to take for their own Lockian conceptions never meant for them, conceptions of contract, rights, and popular sovereignty, much as the proletarian elements of the liberal world did before them. The notion emerges that they have a claim that must be heard. While rarely formulated in these terms, a liberal America begins to question the exclusiveness of the contract or, at least, its implicit ownership of it, a claim which engenders a paternalism that suddenly appears out of place. The human contradictions of the contract become more apparent. What results is a reconsideration of the entire issue of rights, in the world and, as a result, in the United States. American liberalism discovers the basis of its crisis in the world beyond itself, brought about by a struggle against imperial policy that is historic in proportion and effect.

The forces which threaten to contain and throw back the drive for Pax Americana—a drive which finds its origins in early English intrusion into North America—also set in motion economic forces with disturbing consequences for the liberal system. Since the explorations financed by the joint-stock companies of Europe, commercial expansion to the West is a corporate matter, an expression of surplus venture capital seeking investment markets. That such markets are found or created, that they hold out the lure of a greater profit than can be found in domestic investment, provides the economic optimism historically associated with liberal expansion. Traditional support of this phenomenon through the financial and military largesse of a purportedly laissez-faire state testifies that perennial expansion is understood as vital. Because imperialism provides enormous margins of profitability, some of which can be diverted into wages, salaries, and welfare for the population at home, it serves as a crucial buffer against revolutionary demands from within. Imperial policy is the corporate analogue of the welfare liberalism of Mill, attractive to those who maintain his tradition in the modern world.

Having thus mitigated the harshness of financial existence under the competitive market, the great corporations can increasingly ill afford such relative benevolence. Their monolithic presence becomes more oppressive and obvious as the logic of their imperial position intrudes. The "free world"—those realms of the planet where corporate dollars are welcomed and protected—slowly, but inexorably, diminishes. Trade replaces control; the margin of profitability takes a profound drop and must be recovered through the ultimate determination of consumer prices at home. Despite an eager extension of personal credit, this is reflected in a generally declining level of effective income among the metropolitan population.

For a people ideologically nurtured on the notion of capitalist opportunity, this conclusion to the era of imperial expansion, which is largely responsible for economic growth in the American twentieth century, is a traumatic event. In the money markets of the world, the dollar loses value, not as a consequence of an unfavorable balance of trade, but because of an unfavorable balance of payments—the ultimate price for years of shipping wealth out of the country in the form of military personnel, equipment, and operations. What Sweezy terms the "war-preparations economy"[1] —a condition finding its graphic counterpoint in *Nineteen Eighty-Four*—is delicate, and must be kept in careful adjustment. Continual preparation for a war that ideally never comes is disruptive when a large military operation like that in Indochina is dictated by the class position of those who rule. The outflow of wealth eludes control, leading to devaluation and other inflationary effects on the domestic population in an economy already inflationary due to the monopoly power of concentrated industries. Such is the cost of a shrinking imperialism and the military cost of trying to preserve it.

Pressured by an adverse outflow of venture capital, the United States increasingly relies on what it produces best, food and armaments, to maintain a favorable position in the money markets of the world. The people are informed of the financial difficulties of the "nation," the particle of truth residing in the decrease in corporate profitability which characterizes a greater reliance on foreign trade and regulated investment, as opposed to total investment and political and military control. What is in trouble is not the nation, but expected margins of corporate returns.

The initial symptom of disarray, the device whereby most incomes are decreased, is a seemingly intractable, and certainly regressive, inflation, somewhat controllable only in presidential election years, soon accompanied by a recession that attends fiscal and monetary efforts to cool a liberal economy. In a multinational order, where the economics of much of the world are reflections of corporate interests that surpass national identity, to argue that "decisions" by governments on the fringe inflate real prices, that they thereby control the buying power that prices represent, is patently absurd. Still this is propounded in all urgency to a liberal population, a useful claim for those whose power depends upon the relative financial deprivation of others. As with inflation, so with scarcity. Shortages in the United States fundamentally result from control of supply by those with the power to do so. Yet the liberal love affair with scarcity accords credence and reality to the corporate propaganda effort.

That deficit spending, largely a consequence of warfare economics, with its corollary program of foreign aid, pro-

vides a safe and high-yield investment for the giant financial
institutions which dominate and control the money supply
of the country—and much of the world—escapes perception. So does the fact that any loss of consumer demand is
more than recovered by the major corporations, at least for
a while, by raising prices beyond increased costs to national
and international customers and, acting in the capacity of
international bankers, by investments in foreign money
markets; by diverting a greater capital flow to "foreign"
corporations, legally independent but, in fact, subsidiaries
of multinational companies based in the United States; by
an increased reliance on the dollar and profit magnitudes
of war production, magnitudes so vast they are beyond
the appreciation, and even the grasp, of most people.
Finally, the fact that nations not a part of the American
economic domain fail to suffer from the rampant inflation
and persistent unemployment which characterizes nations
within, is little appreciated by a liberal people and, among
those who do, the significance of the phenomenon is fundamentally missed. From the effects of a declining imperialism, multinational corporate interests remain well protected
by the realities of international finance and the impressive
power of the prevailing ideology.

Yet the order is in difficulty. For too long, the corporate
interest is the liberal interest; but from a corporate perspective the allowable margins are now small and, in their own
terms, corporations feel themselves manifestly assaulted
and under pressure. They respond by seeking profit through
techniques and ventures which demonstrate increasingly
less relationship to the production of usable wealth, even as
they work to decrease the real incomes of the American
people, as well as the incomes of a substantial proportion
of the people of the world. Thus, while the enormous and
insured profitability of imperial investment recedes, the
problem of preserving the systemic power arrangements

confronts those who rule, as they desperately attempt to maintain control over the economic perceptions of a liberal population.

All of this impinges on the tacit liberal agreement to deal with income inequality, and to maintain the balance, through the development of economic growth. Those who can least afford it are most hurt by the technique of devaluation and such measures as large agricultural sales to foreign governments in a desperate attempt to correct balance-of-payments difficulties. More people are suddenly alert to the enormous amount of American wealth poured into military production, and to the crucial economic position of such production. They become more acutely aware that it might be used, perhaps against themselves; that the war-preparations economy is a dangerously explosive system and, in any event, as manifested in the balance-of-payments problem, can reach its economic limits.

It is expansion which makes possible the American idea of equal opportunity, and its inherent denial of a social-class system, enabling liberal reformers to avoid the turmoil that must surround any real attempt at economic redistribution, submerging the issue of income equality under an increasing corporate plentitude of wealth and opportunity. Rationalized by the doctrine of manifest destiny, the westward expansion of the American order knew no limits—no physical or human obstacle could long resist as it swept the contours of a continent, spreading beyond the West overland to the West overseas, economically eradicating all pretensions of legal boundaries. Within this movement, the interests and designs of corporate enterprise are the crucial force and motivation. Only the great concentrated firms can afford to indulge in the economics of such grandiose speculation and power. To the extent that liberalism assumes financial expansion, it is inescapably the ideology of corporatism, a corporatism that liberals suddenly recognize, with the anguish of a perception that sees the world falling apart, as the major purveyor of the business ethic that now works to destroy the liberal promise of opportunity that comprises the core of its ideological appeal.

Throughout American economic history, the potential explosion over an invidious distribution of income has been effectively cancelled by the growth of economic opportunity based upon a continual expansion of the totality of wealth to be shared. The success of this idea is the central reason for the failure of socialism in America. And as long as people feel that general abundance is increasing, and that opportunity and a greater real income will result, it continues to be effective. But now opportunity dissolves, its limits reached and, of greater importance, felt to be reached, by a people who begin to perceive the disastrous ramifications of such an event. Even a system of planned obsolescence in consumer goods is of little assistance if people do not have the money to buy what is produced.

Population expansion ends, immigration confined to a trickle so selective and slow that more now leave the country than enter. The birthrate declines in a nation suddenly aware of presumed environmental limits to productivity, while a generally increased affluence works its usual consequence in smaller families. The great movement of overland colonialism reaching to the Pacific closes, leaving only by-passed pockets of isolation still to be settled. The extension of imperialism beyond the continent finds its investment opportunities circumscribed, as those never contemplated by Locke absorb his central principles, according them new interpretations and applications.

As the creation of new markets through expansion of the domestic population declines, as an era of trade replaces a much more lucrative era of investment overseas; a capitalist ideology, predicated on an ethos of expansion or surrender to scarcity, must confront the fact that expansion and opportunity now depend upon a redistribution of personal wealth, precisely that which liberal expansion is designed to avoid. This is deeply unsettling to a people committed to the belief that personal industry and "talent" must result in financial reward, to the notion that the "unfit" should not be well treated, that the fear of poverty and the lure of opulence are necessary because the emotional dimension of man may subvert the dictates of economic reason, that people may cease in their efforts to maximize production if pleasure is too easily and readily attainable. The capital-surplus pressure on major corporations could be eased, though not solved, by a fundamental redistribution that would create new buying power. But the real economic problem is the capitalist ethos itself, an ethos that insists that venture capital that does not maximize profit is inefficient and threatens the balance.

Most Americans agree with this, as they agree that redistribution is not acceptable. Far better to release the unremitting pressure of accumulated venture capital through investment in war production, where obsolescence is controllable and guaranteed, thus creating a market of insatiable opportunity. If this militarizes the American mind, if it induces a warfare frame of reference for all or nearly all acts of the government, if it ensures that a great proportion of productivity is wasted, such price is small enough to circumvent a fundamental disruption of the American way of life. Let the poor work their way into the system as all who are truly American have done: fine advice, perhaps, when opportunity exists; a bit specious when it no longer does.

While general affluence grows, the distribution of wealth in America remains static, a fact which, to be maintained, now amplifies the pressure on a contracting labor market. A large element of the population continues to be poor, and the poor are now unabsorbable into an economy which is losing its elastic ability to expand. The generic inflation of an order where corporations, integrated, conglomerate, and concentric in operation, possess the monopoly power to set their own prices, now amplified by conditions in the greater imperial world, begins to deeply disturb the liberal mind, as the application of the traditional tools of monetary and fiscal policy and antitrust legislation bring no apparent result.

Few Americans understand that the closing off of cheap raw materials from the imperial world, while one basis of inflation, is not the major one; that a system where control of prices and markets is in the hands of a few—and where the few are the pawns of their own assumption of scarcity and are pressured by the accepted motivations of profit and financial greed—is a system which is inherently inflationary. An oligopolistic economics means an inherent tendency for prices to increase; and any regime acting as if a free market exists and which, consequently, does nothing along the lines of controls will, in fact, be engaging in an inflationary policy. Willing to accept government subsidy of "bankrupt" corporations, a view that preserves the illusion if not the reality of "private enterprise," some might agree to price and wage controls and, perhaps, in an extreme extension of liberal sensibilities, to a program of profit controls that might actually lower corporate prices. This would have to accord with a policy of currency stabilization that, to correspond to corporate reality and be effective, must be international in scope. Such a policy, informed by the understanding that an expansion of available money creates more money, is one which would strengthen cheap money but, in so doing, allow for the increase in the money supply necessary for the enhancement of wealth production.

All this, perhaps, is a liberal impossibility. A policy that would interfere with the easy availability of dollars for corporate investment overseas could, of course, expect strong resistance from those who currently wield a disproportionate share of power in the United States. But not even the force of a personally destructive inflation will now bring acceptance of public ownership of basic industries, the only means short of depression of controlling inflation in a system where other attempts at control are subject to sabotage by the "private" power of corporate wealth. The American people are far too liberal for this. So corporate America proceeds, its military foundations starkly revealed by a dramatic increase in the magnitude of concentrated power, since the complex machinery of war can only be produced by those financially and technically organized to do so. It is this, most of all, which now frightens the liberals who bring it about; this and the fact that the system is calculated to frustrate those who find the doors of opportunity closing at the historical moment of their arrival on the economic scene.

The correlation is plain. As corporate power grows, opportunity recedes, particularly the opportunity to freely enter the market with a minimum of financial resource. What opportunity remains is corporate, the concept of the economically independent individual evaporated into a productive form which demands sameness and a totality of commitment to the vague ambitions of an organizational abstraction. Realization that these comprise the conditions of survival in modern America is deeply disorienting for a people acculturated to a liberal notion of opportunity and who now confront the reality of a corporate future. This is a traumatic transformation. Far more than the military immersion in the quagmire of Indochina, it accounts for the profound disillusionment of the generation of the 'sixties—and for the generations that follow, in greater quietude but more realistic comprehension.

As absorption into corporatism becomes the characteristic means of livelihood for the population, as corporate business reacts to the long-range profit squeeze of a declining imperialism with more heavy-handed and obvious behavior at home, as people begin to realize that inflation and unemployment are structural and growing facts of economic existence, the shadows of illusion fade, and the harsh light of actuality intrudes. The changing mood of American liberalism moves from a confidence that history is on its side to a suspicion that the liberal idea, once the assurance of balance, suffers from a historic inability to cope with the modern world. That this is a world which the liberal mind continues to perpetuate because, unable to penetrate the essence of its own system, it can do nothing else, only makes matters more confusing. A sense that the balance is shattered is joined by a feeling that nothing can be done, that alienation from the "system" is the only proper and, indeed, rational response. Participatory democracy—ignorant of its basis in the Jeffersonian idea of local supremacy—is the feeble and inadequate reaction of liberals who think they are "radicals" because they perceive that the financial support necessary to seriously enter larger politics is beyond the reach of nearly all. Liberal optimism, which historically depends upon the reality, or fiction, of opportunity, becomes the despair of a people who perceive themselves cornered by events. Thus does the "crisis" of a prevailing ideology invariably manifest itself.

6. The New Realities of Politics

The view of some liberal economists is that the capitalist stress on productivity camouflages a deeper human concern for a guarantee of employment and, at a more profound level, for economic security in a world of assumed scarcity. In terms of the inner motivations of liberal populations, this is probably the case. But for most philosophers of liberal economics, profit is the key to production and, whatever lies beneath them, the pronouncements of liberal ideology about the right to profit have crucial effect on the outlook and behavior of those subject to their influence.

Dominated by an economic doctrine which formulates its essential promise in terms of the profit to be gained through commodity exchange, Americans long accept alienation from the product of their labor. By ideological definition, they produce for exchange, not use. Work cannot be an end in itself. It must be a means towards the achievement of something separate from the work. The true product of labor becomes the ability to consume the labor of others, attended by the status and power which derive from substantial consumption in a system subsumed by the values of capitalism. As Veblen notes, the more conspicuous and wasteful the consumption, the more invidious the comparison, the greater is the deference gained, and the privilege, prestige, and power accorded. In such manner do the economics of efficiency and reason realize their political and social result. If work is the objective expression of the inner humanity of man, and if a division of labor and alienation from its product is ultimately alienation from this inner humanity, then the price of success in the market system is finally the loss of the self.

Such a system will function only as long as material scarcity is felt as a pervasive force, a literal threat to existence. But as the yield of technological innovation multiplies, as productive man becomes redundant and trivial, a disharmony develops between self-conception and work that must yet be performed. Among the affluent, the concern becomes less a matter of distribution and more a matter of the human realities of productive existence. Alienation from labor has always been a central fact of human existence—predating the market idea which formulates it in terms of commodity production—but awareness of it is an aggregate luxury of the well-off. Once out of the cave, even periodic returns become less tolerable. As a problem, alienation is a problem of the rich or, at least, the relatively rich.

Consciousness of alienation is a revolutionary force which reveals itself incrementally, a symptom of economic surplus which is the foundation of all historic transitions that render established power arrangements less predatory. Those who presently rebel against the values of materialsim—as opposed to those who demand a more equal share of what is materially available—are invariably products of affluent backgrounds in an affluent age, where reasonable wealth is assumed, and where the alienation implicit in working for more is viewed as an unbearable threat to existence as a person. Herein are contained horrendous implications for a system based upon an ethos of productivity, an ethos that yields the abundance which suddenly emerges as the seedbed of disillusion with the order. What is implied—despite the most ingenious efforts of the advertising industry—is an operational limit to consumption; the possibility that people who assume even moderate affluence will resist laboring only to consume more; and, most disturbing of all, that they will increasingly insist upon work that comprises a purpose in itself, and is not merely a means to subsequent rewards. Less apparent in an actual satiability than in a lack of economic urgency, the force of affluence subverts the operative economic values of the liberal system.

The quest for leisure becomes characteristic, perhaps an attempt by human beings to reunite within themselves what is rendered specialized and divided by the demands and conditions of labor, now finding application in the great masses of the population instead of in the traditional few. But its effect is insidious. Not even leisure, which becomes the goal of most labor in America, is enough for an increasing proportion of its people. Leisure allows man to perceive his alienation from his still necessary labor, the growing assumption of abundance intensifying the perception. By permitting perspective on self, leisure constitutes a real danger to a system grounded in the value of production. The yearning for self-actualization, for what is traditionally thought of as the inner harmony of fulfillment, becomes an expression of the developing struggle against the pervasive alienation of people from themselves, a struggle that can only commence as a social force as the perception of abundance is transformed into a more general condition.

Despite the cherished formulations of capitalist economists, which insist that the law of diminishing marginal utility will never allow it, the economic implication of all this is that satiation does exist, that there are limits to material want. This is offensive—and troubling—to those who defend the power arrangements of the status quo, and who comprehend its significance for a corporate order where commodity values comprise the core of what Mosca refers to as "the 'political formula.'"[1] While a friendly state may offset any ultimate contraction in demand through fiscal policy, especially through its purchase of the goods of war, it can do little to safeguard against the political and social significance of such an occurrence. If the value of consumption becomes less important, the power of those who produce suffers. What comes under assault is the economic dimension of liberalism and, as a result, the

great concentrations of corporate power which this dimension produces. A decline in the social power of production
will find its reflection in the complexion of political institutions and in the substance of the law they propound. If
not, if those in authority, in ignorance or desperation, fail
to respond, the result must be widespread alienation from
the political system, an alienation less profound than inner
alienation from self, but far more volatile in its immediate
political potential. A decline in the central economic
assumption of the order—a decline brought about by a perceived affluence—cannot be without political effect.

Power is the problem. The liberal aversion to the idea of
power is so inherent it goes unnoticed, but it produces an
"angle of approach"[2] which loses sight of the issue by
implicitly denying its existence. American conditions have
long allowed the formulators of its operative ideas, and a
population conditioned to these ideas, to indulge in the
fantasy that power can be denied because its translation
into authority will control it. Especially since the New
Deal, such is the aggregate habit of liberal America.

But now the habit weakens. The perception of closing
opportunity, more corporate as it narrows in proportion to
population, inevitably forces awareness of power into the
consciousness of an increasing number of people. The great
liberal response to power, a constitutional philosophy
which denies it, and a pluralism that balances what cannot
be denied, suddenly reawakens, only to appear without
effect when pitted against a corporate octopus of scope
and dimension beyond the classical imagination. A system
of power which allows power to be forgotten is dissolved
or, more accurately, is absorbed by a generic corporatism
it cannot cope with, the conceptions and language of its
ideology skillfully integrated into a propaganda that assures
the exploited that they really rule or, preferably, that no
one does. Suddenly awakened to the fact of power, the
liberal cannot discern the threat he attempts to confront.

But what he can feel as most immediate is the growing tension between an ideology rendered functional by the promise of economic opportunity, stressing the individual, the free market, the denial of power, and the dividing, separating, and checking of what power remains, and a technological system of production which requires concentrated power as an operational necessity; between the liberal idea of man and an organizational conformity; between a constitutional philosophy and a centralized domination at home which, most blatantly, with a callous disregard for human beings worthy of the machine itself, accords direct and indirect military support to tyrannical local regimes in an increasingly desperate attempt to maintain a declining control in the area of its imperial ventures. The contradiction within liberal ideology between the value of production and the value of the person becomes manifest as the organization man, indentured to the corporation, replaceable by others of equal disposition, training, and appearance, replaces the individual of the liberal formulation.

After centuries of harmonious concurrence, liberalism and technological innovation are in conflict. They now enter a struggle for power, awareness of it nurtured by a need for bureaucratic structure that seems to dominate modern existence, and a relative affluence which allows people to glimpse the possibility that material privation need not always be the overriding reality of existence. To note again that liberalism provides the ideological foundation for technological development and the consequent emergence of a corporate civilization that works to destroy the liberal system of power, is only to note the bizarre contradictions of liberalism under technological conditions, a major condition of the age, tearing apart the Newtonian balance. It reflects an ideology out of phase with the realities of power in the modern world.

Whatever the actual configurations of corporate power, whether decision is controlled by a ruling class, a managerial elite, or the plural complexities of a technostructure; whether elements of the ruling stratum are in subtle competition with one another or totally agree, matters little to a population that begins to sense that power is beyond comprehension and control. People need not think in terms of power—although, as its pervasive influence is felt, they do so increasingly—to feel that something has gone wrong with America, that forces unrestrained by balance and reason dictate not only high policy, but the realities of their immediate world. Despite an incessant barrage of propaganda—from mass media to textbooks on government— which assures the majority that they rule their own country, an element of the democratic idea which an elitist liberalism in America traditionally incorporates into the formulations of its own claim and, indeed, its own double-think, Americans increasingly do not believe what they hear and read. They have long understood that America is not democratic; that, appropriately in the liberal order, the many are manipulated by the few. Despite its new intensity, what is new is not the suspicion that the many are ruled by an elite, but the suspicion that the elite is out of control, a feeling of multiplying magnitude that produces despair and a dissolution of liberal control.

It is an inherent contradiction of the productive order that the more material abundance is assumed, the less important it becomes. This incursion on the assumption of scarcity allows the American liberal to finally confront the power realities of the corporate-imperial order which his historic advocation brings into existence. Less do liberals now applaud the pronouncement that America possesses a manifest destiny, a mandate to "civilize" the world by "democratizing" it. More does understanding grow that manifest destiny is an ideological representation of corporate policy; that, within its accepted usage, "democratic" is "liberal," an Orwellian euphemism for the creation of

global areas available for a militarily protected and financially guaranteed flow of surplus capital at a high rate of
return on investment. Liberals also begin to understand
that technological power does not free man but transforms
his bondage into the tense comfort of the organization
man, an interchangeable part, accorded the dignity and self-
respect due all cogs equally in the vast complexity of the
postindustrial machine. Thus do the consequences of abundance proceed.

What centrally disturbs Americans—however unconsciously—is that in a land dominated by capitalist values there is
no capitalism, unless the euphemism of "monopoly capitalism" is seriously considered to represent a type of market
economy, and not the antithesis of the market it actually
is. The ending of the frontier destroys all remaining possibilities for the capitalist order—always agrarian, in fact—
eventuating in the concentrated realities of the technological state. In the agricultural sector, long the bastion of free
enterprise, the few farmers who remain increasingly function as serfs within a complex of control which, as often
as not, is but an element of a conglomerate network of
power. Prices are established by the organized buyers of
the farmer's yield, as are the dictates as to what will be produced. While still frequently well paid, if the allegedly independent farmer resists his assigned function in a greater
planning, he can sell out at a stipulated price, or go into
bankruptcy for a failure of buyers in a supposedly free
market. The absence of an economic West means that even
agricultural America is corporate, that here, as elsewhere,
opportunity demands a submergence of self into the laby-
rinth of bureaucracy, an oppressive reality punctuated by
the absence of classical opportunity, which formulates
success in the person of the independent entrepreneur.
While the persistence of the capitalist ethos in America is
remarkable, it is most fundamentally eroded by the fact of

receding capitalist opportunity within an emerging corporate civilization.

Corporate opportunity—combined with a growing perception of its general decline—represents a disequilibrium, a malfunction of the system which eventually produces a bitter yield of cynicism and despair. Confidence in the liberal idea is further destroyed by an inner contradiction of the order never truly accounted for, but which will no longer remain hidden beneath an apparent harmony. There have always been elements of the population hardly incorporated into the liberal system, never accorded even a minimal share of the wealth, status, and power it distributes. Yet the real political question for a liberal order is not whether all significant factions are satisfied, but whether those factions which are not can reasonably perceive a future where they will be. The great economic promise of the liberal formulation was that the system could eventually accommodate all; that if some had more, each would eventually have enough.

As opportunity closes down, a concurrent demand for entry from more segments of the population becomes abundant and vociferous, due in part to a sense of desperation, but in greater part to a broadening conception of the contract as liberal imperial policy finds significant opposition in the world, and its own citizens increasingly identify with those they view as their compatriots in the imperial areas, as they perceive themselves as victims of the same policy at home. Opportunity declines, and perception of this decline becomes more general and acute, at the precise instant that the pressure for entry becomes greater, more anxious, and more intense. This is no small part of the immediate difficulty of the liberal system, inducing more visible and greater suppression by those who rule, amplifying the sense that power is out of balance.

There is in modern America a dawning conviction that

interests of each, selfishly pursued, do not necessarily yield the welfare of all. Such doubt about the social justification of market philosophy is, of course, nothing new. It is reflected in the Jeffersonian opposition to the policies of the Federalist faction, and in subsequent events which transform opposition to big business into an American tradition. But these were battles joined by those on the outside attempting to gain entrance into an expanding order where entrance was possible. Now the suspicion grows that the system cannot absorb all who demand entrance, that it is structurally incapable of doing so, as those within become fearful that the admission of more will mean the ejection of themselves or—in a more profound dimension of their political anguish—of their children.

The comment of Eugene McCarthy that all liberals can ever agree about is economics contains an element of important truth, if it is understood that the core of such economics is expansion. It reflects an awareness that the dominant ideology—which submerges the ugly issue of income inequality beneath an increasing plentitude of wealth and, more importantly, of opportunity (a position that remains tenable only as long as an increase in the totality of wealth production continues)—now finds itself torn by civil war among its economically diverse adherents. This is symptomatic of an economy that is, or is perceived to be, stabilizing and even contracting, an intolerable condition for a conception of balance which crucially depends upon economic expansion.

Whipsawed by a concurrence of inflation and recession, a capitalist impossibility rendered real when prices are controlled by a concentrated power, anguished by a pervasive pressure on income and a growing sense that economic expansion and opportunity have ended in America, confused by an amplified perception of abundance, a liberal

people begins to take critical and cynical notice of a bureaucratized reality that has no place in the ethos of liberalism;
of the inconsequence of the person when arrayed against a
system that, somehow, has become inherently corporate. As
economic pressure continues, consciousness slowly emerges,
and phrases strange to the political vocabulary are heard.
Liberals begin to wonder how America got where it is, if
that to which they willingly assented for so long can be
rectified, if the versions of tyranny in a corporate world,
warned of by Huxley, Kafka, and Orwell, and advanced by
Skinner,[3] can be averted—if there is still any possibility for
the Newtonian balance.

If the liberal attempt is, indeed, in crisis, if its political
inspiration is to fail, it will be a failure of ironic magnitude.
As the people of the most liberal society in history are
beset by pressures and events that force them to recognize
the inner contradictions of their own system, much of the
world is absorbing the Lockian ethos, not necessarily in
terms of the right to property, but certainly in terms of
popular sovereignty, a contracted and constitutional authority, and the conception of rights itself. While the liberal
idea seeps by painfully slow osmosis throughout the globe,
the paramount liberal nation finally confronts the interior
realities of its essential ideology, struggling to decipher the
inner dilemmas of its existence.

Never has a people been so liberal. Never has a liberal
Volksgeist so dominated the reflexes of a nation. Never has
a population been so saturated with the rational elitism
of Locke, with the doctrine and theory of the market
philosophy. The crisis of the American condition, whether
articulated as a crisis of "authority," "legitimacy," "confidence," basic "Americanism," or "power," is inherently a
crisis of liberalism. It is a crisis of root and language, of
ideology and world view, of the very terms of the order. In

the final analysis, it is a crisis of the Newtonian balance that always comprised the central promise of what a liberal America was about. A civilization constructed upon this conception will redeem itself, or fail, only in terms of its own commitment. Liberal ideology will dictate what the possibilities for America are.

As is always the case, few are in conscious rebellion against the system. But the causes of their discontent manifest a new condition, a condition of bureaucratized power set against a counterpoint of affluence that frees the energies for considerations beyond the material. If some in America must subsist on dog food or its equivalent, this does not reflect on the abundance which is available, but on a liberal distribution; which is a disgrace. Despite periodic reversions to the rhetoric and policies of Social Darwinism—reversions made possible by voting patterns produced by a fear of the poor—the politics of affluence press rapidly forward, applauded by a people born to the productive ethos of liberal ideology. The basis and the fact of abundance cannot tolerate the operative continuation of the principles of Social Darwinism or, for that matter, of a reform liberalism, principles which draw their economic justification from the assumption of scarcity.

Thus, while the economics of abundance are inescapably corporate, the material yield they create transforms American expectations in a manner highly disturbing to corporate control. As profit-margins are threatened by a shrinking imperial domain, while corporate managers opt for immediate gains in profitability as, concerned about stockholder reactions, they feel time is no longer on their side, a new expectation at home permits only a certain degree of passing the financial burden onto the established orders of those who work. The system of internal distribution which corporate liberalism long employs to avoid a decent policy on incomes cannot simply be dissolved when the luxury of its continuation becomes less affordable. Where affluence is established, pressure for it to continue will be great, its assumption becoming a potent political fact; and where affluence is broadly visible, those yet to possess it will increase their demands to do so. This is true of the world, but it is most immediately true of America.

As abundance becomes an assumed condition, its political consequences magnify. Nothing is more destructive to the ethos of capitalism, with its flow of wealth to those deemed most crucial to production, attended by the status and power that accompanies such wealth, than a condition of abundance where material possession and those who finance its production, who control what Macpherson describes as "the means of labour,"[4] begin to lose central importance. That such transformation of values is first manifested in the affluent and educated young is more than understandable. It is highly significant for a technological order that requires precisely such people for its own continuation.

Thus does the liberal become "radicalized," a strange "radical" who seeks a return to the past balance of the order. It is the educated young whose reactions lead, because it is they who are reared on the assumption of affluence, and who find little commitment to the justifications of the warfare state. They suffer least from what Galbraith propounds as "the depression psychosis,"[5] the deep fear that a poverty long gone will somehow reappear. It is the young, lacking experience with scarcity, a generation, as C. P. Snow suggests, which uniquely thinks of itself as a generation apart,[6] to whom the old slogans sound most empty and absurd.

The contention of MacLeish is that the despair of American liberalism is a result of its "anti-communist" and reactionary stance in the world; that the failure of the American dream is a failure of its foreign policy. "It is not because we are too comfortable that the dream has left us."[7] From this, it is a small extrapolation to find that what set young people into overt opposition to the "system" was an unpopular military involvement in Southeast Asia, that a change in foreign policy will transform all; and with this, most liberals will agree.

But as foreign policy cannot be abstracted from the internal conditions of the nation it represents, so the essence of the generational problem is much deeper than this, and ultimately more dangerous to the power of a liberalism that prefers to ignore it. Disenchantment with the war and, by extension, the military establishment and foreign policy in general, is effect not cause, manifested in, but not created by, a sudden inability of the corporate state to successfully merchandise a war to those called upon to fight it. Certainly, the same appeal, replete with slogans of "anti-communism" and "national defense," was always sufficient before. Now all it achieves is intensification of suspicion, of a political malaise disturbing in the enormity of its reach.

The realities of the war in Indochina were little different than the realities of previous American involvements. What is different is that the facts became revealed, not because they were unusual, but because the objects of state propaganda—within and without the media—were different. At issue is not the idealism of the antiwar movement—which, despite the pundits of retrospect, epitomized much of it—but why a normal resistance to being drafted was not subject to dissolution through the standard appeals. What changed were not the techniques of merchandising but the targets of their nationalistic propaganda. That the draft could only work, and then not too well by, in fact if not in law, exempting the educated is revealing. So is current pressure for an all-volunteer military, which will release the affluent and the educated from the struggle to retain control of a dissolving imperial domain. The present resistance to military service reflects a generational distrust of the processes and institutions of liberal government, containing implications far more significant than might be apparent.

It is a symptom of the liberal crisis that becomes less isolated. As indicated by the evidential yield of polling techniques, those no longer young slowly follow. "The rest of the country was slowly but surely coming around to . . . broader views on a whole host of subjects. . . . The major impact of young people was being felt with increasing weight in the areas of their greatest social concerns: on the race issue, on environmental controls and the quality of life, and on the responsible use of U.S. power around the world."[8] Seemingly led by a generation less experienced and knowledgeable than itself, a substantial segment of the American population is reluctantly forced to reconsider the realities of an economic order that produces the symptomatic problem of a liberal nation, the steady erosion of the Newtonian balance.

What gradually comes home to liberal perception is that the great worlds of the economic and the political no longer balance each other because they are each other. Inequality in the economic sphere is increasingly seen as maintained by its counterpart in the political which, far from contending against economic power, is its partner in domination, cloaking corporate decision in an authority it would otherwise lack. That such is the traditional contention of socialism disturbs fewer people in liberal America, not because they are getting "soft" on "communism" and other "red" ideas, but because of a transition in liberal perceptions of reality. The major bastion of balance—the natural bifurcation of the economic from the political—is seen to be violated ever more brutally as it becomes plain that the trickle-down doctrine of the corporate powerful controls the economic policies of the state, replacing the balance and opportunity of competing entrepreneurs with the domination of a modern corporatism. Liberals even come to suspect that those who most resisted the New Deal are its greatest beneficiaries, that, indeed, many of them tacitly supported it while offering ideological homage to resistance.

Thus, while the population is still generally placated by the opiates of the order, it is no longer as content as before, as external pressures on the imperial dimension of the system are felt at the center and passed down among the many, where a heightened consciousness, emerging from this and a concurrent abundance, insists upon deeper penetration into the realities of the national existence. As the virus of discontent spreads, a population whose ultimate policy is balance finds itself arrayed against a highly organized and bureaucratic force which fills the void of power, taking unto itself the authority of the state while pursuing purposes manifestly its own. Understanding of power grows, as does the conviction that in some way it must be dealt with. As the liberal mind slowly admits to the presence of power, the problem of restraining it is formulated in traditional terms. But it becomes apparent that all potential force for restraint is now absorbed into the corporate basis of modern existence, and a desperate search for power to control power—for a potential locus of countervailing power—becomes the initial conception of the liberal response.

III

RENEWAL

$E = MC^2$

Albert Einstein

7. Science

That technological production demands education and youth is an obvious fact which, apparently too obvious, is dismissed as politically unimportant by the propounders of the liberal position. America is a nation of Rube Goldbergs, its facility with machines and machine tools the envy of the world and the basis of much of its power within it; and machines are predicated upon technological understanding, and technology is ultimately dependent upon the intellectual abstractions of scientific theory. But liberals who do recognize the vital role of educated imagination in the scientific discovery which underlies a technological civilization do so with little enthusiasm and, indeed, despair. The "scientific establishment" is perceived as a cabal of "new mandarins,"[1] devoid of political vision, agents of the prevailing order who form the connecting tissue between corporate business and the state and universities, which are merely shadow elements of its organic system. Universities, wherein most engaged in doing "scientific" work congregate, are collectors and suppliers of necessary data—reservoirs of specialized information compiled on order of its corporate directors—and the trainers of the corporate young. As a potential basis of balance, the history of the "scientific" establishment is one of eager complicity with forces which now compose a tyrannical complex of power. Few liberals think of science as a political force and, for those who do, its record is shabby and, as a possible locus of contending power, not worthy of serious consideration.

But what is ignored is consciousness, a developing understanding that the edifice of technology totally depends upon a rapid and continual flow of scientific discovery. As this fundamental fact permeates the awareness of those involved in such discovery, the suggestion of a political

91

awakening infiltrates the realm of science. What more perceptive practitioners of business and government have long realized slowly dawns upon those who do science, who, beginning to comprehend that they are crucial to the order, manifest behavior more cantankerous and strange than usual. Thus are the first symptoms of consciousness of power expressed, a consciousness which, if actually attained, will reflect the productive realities of a technological age instead of those of a past which the failure of the liberal imagination will not allow it to escape.

Fundamental and necessary differences exist between the perceived interests of those in pursuit of wealth—the owners and salesmen of America—and those engaged in scientific search and explanation. Managerial concerns about productivity are distinct from the concerns of science, as is the perspective of the myriad human composition of the "technostructure." None of the liberal perspectives on power can account for the possibility that science might have a vital political role, because none can accept the possibility that science is a force separable from the ruling stratum, whatever theory of that stratum is being advanced. One exception is Galbraith, who, borrowing from Veblen,[2] is well known among liberals as the originator of the concept of the "technostructure." But this is an extended element of his thought, widely ignored by his liberal colleagues and, when acknowledged, misunderstood or dismissed as naive. Yet a failure to understand science as a potential countervailing force is a failure to comprehend the dominant political reality of the twentieth century.

The concept of a postindustrial order is variously defined according to general level of education, general level of income, or by the fact that service workers comprise a greater proportion of the labor force than production workers. All of these criteria describe corporate America. But the basic characteristic of a postindustrial system is found in the changing realities of power arrangements as they become distinct from those of the industrial age.

A postindustrial nation is technological in its pervading characteristic—the abundant flow and application of physical invention. It succeeds only if that upon which it is constructed, scientific discovery and the necessary organization of human beings, is adequately maintained and advanced. If the central necessity of technological production is science, so is it the essential feature of the technical planning necessary to corporate economics, a planning which produces the enormous financial success of the business corporation and—according to the laws of social existence—an order dominated by the values and motivations of corporate enterprise. Despite proclamations of "free enterprise," and the other assurances of systemic propaganda, organized and expensive research is the most crucial need of a technological mode of production. The economic demand of the age becomes a demand for educated intelligence and perception; for minds trained to technology and, importantly, to the larger conceptions behind discovery and organization, the milieu of scientific theory wherein "technology" functions.

If power attends that factor of production most crucial and in shortest supply, it is no longer land, labor, or even capital that fits this description. It is not even the organized technical knowledge characteristic of the technostructure. The decisions permeating the order become more complex, and the reality of power flows to those who possess the educated vision to grasp the theories and formulations which yield social and technical reason in the modern world. As the necessity of scientific comprehension sinks deeper into the corporate structure, its influence is increasingly felt and pervasive, and discovered as necessary to technological application. And, as the fact of power yields —as it eventually must—an awareness of power, a new polit-

ical force is born. Enhanced by the fact that the central
artifact of technology, the machine, increasingly automates
production itself—rendering mundane functions unneces-
sary and, indeed, encumbering, demanding ever greater
levels of education in those who produce—a transformation
in the loci of power, however resisted, is inevitable. As the
scientific realm, and its corollary of educated technicians,
slowly becomes aware of its real power, the fact that effective science is a function of widespread formal education
also becomes more vitally understood.

The rapid growth of scientific organization, from the
specialized societies of the nineteenth century into a pro-
lific and well-financed international power which now permeates the university world, vital to the corporate system
and its governmental reflection, is nothing short of historically remarkable. That university organization, however
bureaucratic in the most pejorative sense of the term, is the
social seedbed of a scientific civilization, becomes more
plain, and is finally assumed. The attitudes of scientific
understanding, the attitudes of search and speculation,
come to permeate all disciplines within the university complex. The interests of science and the educational establishment coalesce and, despite vociferous denials from within
and attempts to trim the development of this growing
combination from without, their interests necessarily become the interests of the order itself. Within the nexus of
science and the university exists a new form of power,
enormous in its potential magnitude and effect, a combination of economic forces that, within a liberal conception of
politics, is best understood as the faction of science. What
is most necessary for a liberalism that despairs of the balance is not so much a new reality, but a deeper perception
of the realities which comprise a postindustrial system; a
consciousness of the organized power already at the dis-
posal of the faction of science.

The evidence suggests that these new elements of power are becoming understood and beginning to find expression. Those educated to the scientific outlook find themselves in increasing conflict with those who would return to the power configurations of managerialism, or an older capitalism, armed with the fictions of a previous and more desirable age which always attend a fundamental transition of power. Despite the best efforts of a multifaceted "McCarthyism" to discredit and dismantle the educational establishment, it multiplies in scope and importance—mute testimony to the productive facts of the modern world. A developing disgust with the endless struggle to contain the emergence of China as a world power eventuates in a war resistance that, for the first time in American history, finds its inception and organizational basis within science and the universities, a resistance that renders the war distasteful and finally impossible. To attribute this event to the size of the student population and its unwillingness to serve in an unpopular war in Indochina is to ignore questions of why it attains such size, and why the war became unpopular, questions which even national and state administrations, bent upon destroying the "subversive" influence of "misguided" knowledge, must eventually confront. What the success of the antiwar movement represents is a growing awareness of power, a symptomatic dropping away of the fear to act and, most critically, a broad awakening to the possibility that the interests of corporate business and the interests of the scientific faction are ultimately not the same.

That the actions of those engaged in scientific work betray a common trait of pursuing interests that scientists perceive as their own—as contrasted to some conception of the universal interests of mankind—that their actions reveal the usual mixture of nobility, deceit, and self-serving that attends human behavior, does not mitigate their political

importance. The liberal argument for balance neither requires nor expects the moral, rational, and selfless temperament of the philosopher king to typify the membership of
any certain faction within the order. A liberal view of man
cannot even conceive of this possibility, the entire idea of
balance flowing from the assumption that the existence of
such people is impossible. Thus the penchant for liberal
intellectuals to attack the scientific establishment because
its members are as human as anyone else is accurate, but it
misses the point. It reveals, once again, that modern liberals
are out of touch with their own tradition.

What does not miss the point is that the liberal idea seeks
a restraint on power which can only result from the reality
of contending factions, equal and opposite, none of which
are necessarily in rational pursuit of the higher good of balance itself. It is not a drawback that men pursue their own
interests; indeed, it is important that they do—as long as
they perceive them differently. It does not matter that men
are socially wrong, as long as they do not agree. The importance of the emerging power of science is not that it is
"better" than the prevailing power—although it may be—
but that it cannot be absorbed by a technological system
which absorbs all else. Scientific theory is the foundation
of modern technology and, consequently, the modern
world. It can be destroyed as an autonomous force only if
the technological mentality wants to endure the collapse of
its own system.

Thus do the "new mandarins" contain within themselves
the possibility of restraining the dominance of capitalist
values within the corporate structure and the order it typifies, a dominance which will continue only if the faction of
science fails to attain full consciousness of the power and
purpose it represents. This power, devolving from the
simple fact that science is necessary, is enhanced by organi-

zation that already exists, by the erosion of necessary drudgery and the concurrent expectation of affluence, and by the insistent demand for an ideology that speaks to needs beyond those served by the ethos of wealth accumulation—a demand which, in its central implications, is really a demand for an economic reconstruction of the liberal idea. The essential problems of the age do not revolve around the need to maximize production in a system suffering the pressure of material scarcity, but around the necessity for a more equitable distribution of a distinctly possible abundance.

If there exists a correspondence between affluence, leisure, and speculation, the forces of the scientific outlook become enhanced by the material consequences of technology itself. As man dares to conceive of freedom from economic concerns, he is disposed to larger considerations of aesthetics and existence both within and beyond the self, including the monumental issue of a global and domestic poverty surrounding the relative affluence of a few. Such is the tendency of consciousness within the technological system. It is likely to slowly become the tendency of the rest of the world, much of which adopts the liberal formulation as it begins to emulate its productive achievements. As affluence increases, man begins to see his interests in larger terms. The human disposition towards abundance is a revolutionary power which, yet to become fully conscious, gropes for leadership, a leadership that science, because of its inherent perspective and the strategic position it occupies within the order of technology, is uniquely situated to provide.

Yet those who urge a return to the market ethos may prevail. There exist demagogues who would gather the winds of fear and who, in sincerity or cynicism, could succeed to the power of ignorance, to the outrage of a frustrated liberalism too locked in classical perceptions to break free of the dogmas of its own past. Then, what Mumford refers to as "the failure of nerve"[3] will fully prevail.

Many ideas of contradiction are attributed to Marx, but the Marxist version has theoretical application only within orders of reality, not between them.[4] It follows that the "contradiction" between ideology and the mode of production in corporate America is not really a contradiction in the Marxist sense, although those claiming to write in this tradition often refer to it as such. But there is a Marxist contradiction within an ideology committed to the rights of man and the right to profit, within a class structure that desires to sell commodities to a population which it must economically decimate, within relationships of production that can only survive on the basis of a concurrence of poverty and affluence.

To the extent that liberalism can recover the confidence of its own population, it must most immediately resolve the tension between the capitalist promise of equal opportunity and a system within which opportunity was always far less than the ideological claim, and which now closes off with frightening acceleration. Confronted by the ending of geographic and population colonialism, by a world less susceptible to the brutal requirements of imperialism, and by a technological explosion that renders the cultivated skills of great aggregates of people productively useless, the liberal order faces the impossibility of its central economic claims. Liberal love of technology—finding its etiology in the assumption of scarcity—now flies in the face of a commitment to opportunity which is crucial to the success of its own idea. As those with most to lose become fearful that the demands of those who want more cannot be met, their power becomes crass and obvious, permitting more to comprehend that it is not the market, but the corporate rich, who rule. Those who contend that America is a corporate civilization are suddenly heard. Awareness grows that the imbalance of the system is a fact which the illusion of opportunity can no longer deny. A perceived disappearance of opportunity becomes the immediate cause of liberal disarray.

If "revolution" is understood as a transformation of values and attitudes on a mass scale, resolution of the liberal crisis requires revolutionary change in the concept of opportunity itself. It is one thing to economically subjugate those already poor; it is quite another to deprive a people conditioned to relative opulence and the promise of more. History, as Heilbroner points out, can be ignored for only so long as it appears to be on one's side.[5] It can no longer be ignored by America. The implications of the end of liberal opportunity become rampant; the anger of an affluent people perceiving new deprivations becomes manifest. Liberal opportunity, wherein each possesses an equal right to demonstrate how economically unequal he really is, can only succeed when many think they can win, and when those who lose find it reasonable to aspire to a new opportunity to reenter the competition. This is the basis of what Wills depicts as the society of "earners"—the liberal society. Short of income redistribution, it requires an absolute constancy of economic expansion.

But such a vision of society cannot maintain even the pretense of reality within an order where, in relation to aggregate population, few win, where the productive mode is characteristically cooperative and not competitive, and where, most critically of all in an era of imperial decline and growing automation, opportunity is in absolute retreat. These are facts which demand that the liberal idea of economic equality be replaced by the democratic idea that all must enjoy an equal right, not to be the best among others, but to find the best within themselves, the creative, aesthetic, and human dimensions of their personalities. The difference is profound because it separates economic man from man *qua* man. It is a difference that is vital—not only in ethos and in its inherent definition of what is valued—but in its effect on the economic institutions necessary to maintain the system such a fundamental shift will produce. This represents a truly new condition. Its societal attainment initially requires an understanding that the perspective of science is not the perspective of the order that creates it as a social force.

This becomes manifest in a matter of immediate economic importance. If a receding imperialism and the necessities of technological production close down opportunity within a system steeped in the expansionist values of capitalism, no such effect is experienced within science and by those trained to the more sophisticated application of its technological possibilities. As economic opportunity generally declines, the social demands for scientific investigation enormously increase, demands less for toil than for work, for a less one-dimensional, specialized, and divided form of labor, that will allow at least some objective expression of the inner self. What is in question is not the fundamental need for scientific investigation and speculation, but the financing of its efforts. Since the corporate state under pressure becomes less interested in such financing, a prosperous population becomes an economic necessity for the faction of science. A modern science, highly organized and, therefore, highly social, begins to comprehend its political connection to the enhancement of opportunity in the larger society. Indeed, as corporate America finds its interest in a global ignorance that allows the sale of its product to those who cannot produce it themselves, science begins to find its interest in an expansion of educated intelligence to the greater world.

Deep within the structure of technological America, vital to its continued existence, science becomes the only organized force capable of responding to increased demands for opportunity under modern conditions. Protected by the corporate form which gives it organizational shape and substance, and by the material abundance it produces, the faction of science gathers its strength by confronting the realities of its position. As they become aware of the problems attendant to power, its members begin to understand that expanding economic security enhances their social function and improves their political situation. The willingness to limit opportunity which now controls the logic of monopoly capital is increasingly unacceptable as it comes into notable conflict with interests of their own, interests which are suddenly and plainly separable from those of the still dominant exploitive sectors of the corporate order. The conflict of values between the research staff and the acquisitive personnel of the modern corporation is well documented and well known to those within corporate circles. Now curtailment of opportunity looms as an immediate threat to the scientific faction, and the clash becomes more general and intense. A quiet struggle for control of corporate policy, long imminent, commences. Organized science, the scion of corporate liberalism, cloaked in the political respectability of the corporate order itself, enters a phase of vital conflict with the values that accord the power it already possesses.

8. The Politics of a Scientific Civilization

Corporate wealth allows what capitalist scarcity cannot. It enhances the freedom of science to act politically. Only on the foundation of economic security can the democratic idea of opportunity become real; and only on the basis of a conditioned assumption of abundance can such security, which is ultimately a psychological state, actually exist. The emergence of an ideology which separates rational planning for growth from considerations of corporate profitability can, paradoxically, only occur in a corporate civilization that produces sufficient societal and personal affluence to mitigate and eventually destroy the atavistic motivation of financial anxiety. Ideological emergence is measured only in terms of historic time, the discrete events of its formation difficult to discern. But a reality that renders production less important as it becomes more plentiful, the essential contradiction of the corporate order, patently establishes the conditions where the values of the cash nexus, which are the traditional basis of its success, must be replaced with the values of science.

Yet the notion of science as a political force is not real to liberals or, indeed, to anyone within the accepted spectrum of political speculation. That modern liberals, even while seeking the plurality of factions, reject the idea of science as political, is to be expected: despite vociferous denials of the existence of power, even liberals do not like to lose it, especially since admitting the fact involves a recognition that the system that once bestowed it has evaporated. In a similar fashion, socialists must realize that a corporate order saturated in capitalist values is not a capitalist system. Few elements of the liberal population are less critical of "private" corporate power, few are more caught by a false consciousness of loyalty to firm or industry, than those who appear to fit the traditional description of proletarian—not surprising in light of the fact that their welfare is directly connected to corporate success, to the profitable economics of warfare and pollution that keeps them in a vulnerable financial position. They are easily automated out of existence and, as Deutscher suggests, the position of organized labor in the Soviet Union, as a possible alternative, is not greatly envied by workers in Western Europe[1] and, by extension, in the United States. Those who rely on the economic effects of a declining imperialism to bring this "proletariat" to a spontaneous consciousness fail to consider the functional necessities of technology in any resultant system, and the attendant problem of controlling power within it.

If the bourgeois consciousness of America is a reflection of liberal opportunity; if, following Hartz, socialism is not a reaction to the coming of capitalism, but to the concentrated power of an earlier feudalism—or, more accurately, dynasty—then the time for socialism in America may have arrived, produced by the concentrated power of a corporate world. Yet, while traditional socialism can resolve the difficulties of inflation and distribution, the enormous bureaucratic power which is inherent in the technological character of modern production remains a pervasive reality, one that must be confronted if a people acculturated to the ethos of a distrust of power are to be influenced. Those who look to proletarian revolution, and who see nothing positive in science, might recall that Marx conceives of the proletariat as the catalyst of revolution precisely because it is vital to the characteristic production of the capitalist stage, the basic production that all other production depends upon; that it is inherently organized by the organization of work itself, and is finally alienated by the domination of a class which robs it of the yield of its own productivity and the power of and over its own labor.

These are the factors that render the notion of "proletariat" more than a romantic abstraction, and they are factors which increasingly describe the scientific establishment in the modern world. It would be well for the devotees of "scientific socialism" to consider—as Marx does—the revolutionary potential of science itself.

Those who advocate a "revolutionary" populism might recognize that most "popular" revolutions are led by an educated elite, that the role of leadership in America is to bring people to understand that capitalist man never was free, but the anxious prisoner of an outmoded idea; that freedom requires a condition where the economic security of each is assured; and that a system dominated by warfare economics does not provide this, that such a system yields not protection from without, but the end of liberal opportunity within. The dictum of Lenin that revolution requires a revolutionary theory is not easily dismissed. A notion of leadership may offend the populist prejudice that political wisdom naturally emanates from the masses; but, unfortunately, in a world that is complex and removed from the immediate perceptions of most people, leadership is a political necessity.

It is the faction of science, grounded in the organization of the university, that represents the real possibility of such leadership. This may suggest an elitist paternalism. But if the real idea of science and the university is not served, if the power of its combination falls into the hands of "educated" martinets who, in a logical extension of the ethos of the "earner," eagerly pursue a system of supposed "merit," it nonetheless represents a rational elitism that attracts a liberal people. Despite its role as a major purveyor of the "new American celebration,"[2] as the agent of corporate interest and perception, the complex of the university is pressured by the demands of a scientific mentality within, a pressure that ultimately represents the organization of countervailance and the power of a new perspective.

The radical critique is correct when it identifies the universities as fundamental to the order, but—preoccupied with the "conservative" propensities of many scientists—it fails to recognize the radical importance of the emergence of science and its inherent connection to university organization. Yet, transformations of basic power relationships are always unnoticed until the reality of change is firmly established. "Men become fully conscious of what they have done only some centuries after they have done it."[3]

As art discovers a harmony which is heretofore undiscovered, rendering it accessible to the consciousness, the inner aesthetic of science demands that investigation pursue the symmetrical nature of the event. Arrangements of political power are the historical reflections of technological invention. But it is the scientific search for harmony which controls the limits of technology and, as a consequence, those considerations of power which dominate human existence.

The essential character of any civilization depends upon the condition of its scientific understanding. Yet certain factors distinguish the contemporary liberal order from those which historically precede. Never have the core values which cement a system been so dependent upon technological virtuosity—a virtuosity which finds its presupposition in a science that is materialistic in the empirical demands of its evidence but idealistic in the demands of its method, in the imaginative abstractions of scientific theory. More directly political is the fact that a science which grounds modern technology must be organized; that those who do science must increasingly work together, and that out of the organized conditions of work comes the organization of politics. Like any organized force which possesses a past, science has frequently resisted innovation and discovery; yet, because of the inherent demands of its methodology, the commitment to reality has ultimately prevailed. Now this methodology becomes a crucial necessity to the values of the order, and its consequent organized nature transforms science into a vital political force for the first time in history. Modern liberal civilization is a scientific civilization, and this fundamental reality, however unrecognized, however camouflaged by its technological product, finally determines the configurations of potential power within the system.

A technological nation cannot exist without organized intelligence, and intelligence possesses a disturbing penchant for intruding into the realms beyond its "professional" province. Especially is this true of the theoretical intelligence necessary to inquiry, as distinct from the intelligence of technological application. The physicist is commonly more "radical" than the engineer. The concern of some that such people are dangerous—that, like Cassius, they think too much—is well founded. But despite the most imaginative efforts of a Red-scare politics always inherent in American liberalism, their emergence as a crucial and organized force cannot be contained short of an unacceptable return to a system inordinately less productive. Within the core of the postindustrial order, the power of countervailence exists; an emerging faction which contains the potential to lead an ultimate battle over the policies of opportunity against those who presently control them.

Yet inside the bureaucratic complexity of science and the university, those who think about its social function do not see it as a force for ideological change, thus betraying a liberal disposition for the possessors of power to deny it— even to themselves. And such denial seems to make sense. As in all politics, the intra-politics of science contains forces of division and consolidation which operate concurrently in a quiet struggle for supremacy. Rivalry for financing and control among the "real sciences," the social sciences, and the "humanities"; among academic disciplines and departments; among and between individual scholars and administrators, is an apparent symptom of disarray. That the abundant flow of money from the corporate state into the research function of the university is all but totally channelled to the "hard" sciences reveals that the dominance of corporate America remains well entrenched. The technical mind cannot understand science, although it thinks it does, finding its link to technology obvious, its connection to the "software" of philosophy and humanism obscure. This same failure of understanding controls the funding of social "investigation," where those "scientifically" supportive of the war and social policies of the state become the major recipients of its largesse. All of this disperses the potential power of the scientific faction as a countervailing force, and strengthens the view that science is simply the handmaiden of established corporate control.

But other realities, which are centripetal in effect, begin to solidify science and its attendant university organization as a force in the order. Intentions of a bureaucratic mentality controlling the flow of public and "private" money notwithstanding, as soon as the university takes control, possession becomes vague. Financing moves to people likely to identify with the search for truth, who must, at least, appear to manifest a concern for the larger interests of a scholarly community; rendering them analogous to the directorate of a corporate firm which thinks beyond the interests of its company to those of the industry and, indeed, the system. Beyond this exists the pressure of those necessary to technological production who, passing through the university as students, and expressing the attitudes of an assumed affluence, demand more attention be paid to the greater concerns of the world. They are eagerly joined by younger faculty, their peers of not so long ago, and grudgingly deferred to by older members of the academy who, supposedly set in the traditional arrangements of academic

power, find themselves agreeing more often than is comfortable.

Most important of all, a sense of common interest accel-
erates as the economics of imperial retreat intrude upon
the academy, the technical mentality of those who control
the financial policies of the state enhancing its discontent
through an inability to comprehend not only the strong
intellectual dependencies and attachments that exist, often
in strange configurations, but the desire for mutual protection that their policies induce. No longer can the scientific
world feel safely a part of the corporate system. Now it
must reach beyond itself as it slowly realizes its vital stake
in the broadscale opportunity that corporate America is
increasingly anxious to suppress. As always, power becomes
aware of itself in reaction to power grossly imposed.

Crucially, this takes place in a condition not of scarcity
but of abundance. Still, the assumption of scarcity in liberalism is so strong that it renders abundance as a social fact
almost impossible for the liberal mind to comprehend, or
even to bear, while it remains simultaneously useful for the
maintenance of the present relations of power. Although
the problem of shrinking resources is real, the alacrity of
the American liberal in incorporating it into his perspective,
joyously, as it were, is revealing of a deep need for the concept of scarcity in a world wherein he can find ideological
comfort. This is even manifest in the ideas of certain
American "radicals" who, never realizing they are liberals,
saturate their "Marxism" in a liberal scarcity, perceiving
revolution as the consequence of poverty, not wealth. But
it is perception of surplus which comprises the historic
force of revolution. "Abundance is the basis of the whole
structure of the revolution and of Marxist thinking within
the revolution,"[4] not only because Marx conceives abundance as necessary to new means and modes of production
and the emergence of man, but because he understands that

it is the ultimate reality of the force of surplus, and the political intelligence to understand who is expropriating its yield, that makes revolutionary change possible. But surplus must first be perceived as a systemic reality, and, under modern conditions of production, this perception cannot devolve from abject ignorance and poverty, but only from a necessary level of economic sophistication that depends upon education and some experience with affluence.

The force of surplus dawns upon the scientific faction and congeals its potential power. It suddenly finds itself faced with dire warnings of deprivation in the midst of a plenty that cannot be hidden. It becomes pressured by the young and, in deeper agony, by the parents of the young, who find the exhortation of government at all levels, and the advice of "prestigious" commissions, that their future is best served by training for manual labor, disturbingly unacceptable, especially when accompanied by an implicit understanding that a decent existence in a technological world is accorded only to the educated. Along with a growing proportion of the unemployed and the "unemployable" —especially the unemployed or "underemployed" educated who took seriously the liberal idea—they comprise a growing and angry force for change in a system that has betrayed them. Expectations are not so easily turned off. The ideology of opportunity will not dissolve because the elitist predilections of those in power prefer ignorance and poverty as techniques of maintaining the social vestiges of a declining imperial system, and the graduated failure of equity it systematically represents. An unrequited demand for opportunity in the midst of a perceived opulence, if not attended, contains the potential for an actual revolution in America. Like it or not, science is tied to these forces of liberal disappointment. In the final analysis, consciousness is imposed by the realities of factional politics.

Scientific and corporate power are concurrent reflections

of liberal opportunity. Now those who control the imperial corporations and their attendant state—subservient to the traditional values of profit—see their interests best served not by the expansion of opportunity, but by its curtailment. Yet the values and power of science have a vital stake in its extension. When surplus exists while imperial profitability recedes, the vast differences between the interests of corporate capital and the interests of the scientific community become more sharply drawn and increasingly plain precisely over the issue of expanded opportunity. New political combinations are in order.

In struggling to educate the population to new values, the faction of science begins to educate itself to the realities of the liberal order. Through the process of political engagement, those in science learn that a liberal politics is a politics of alliances; that factions available for new combinations are those not content with their current share of the power totality. They come to realize that the field of liberal politics must be expanded; that political opportunity must be created because allies are required if the power imbalance which corrupts the order is to be dissolved, if the enhancement of liberal economic opportunity and democratic opportunity to find the inner self is to become the basic policy of the state. Science as a political force must become greater than itself in an expanding political universe, its natural allies found among those who currently possess little power.

It is nothing less than classically liberal to perceive science as a force emerging as an articulated political faction, centered in the great universities and within the crucial interlock of the corporations and the state, its influence on events already vital, if largely unremarked. But the political potential of a humane science, which understands the humanistic foundations of its own existence, may reach beyond a liberal factionalism. Science is predicated on the values of inquiry and the open mind, not on the values of the market—although the growth of science as an organized force is historically associated with the market. Corporate business cannot really confine the yield of investigation and the values that control it. These are contagious, especially as great numbers of the population are systematically exposed to them, with college degrees an occupational necessity and "continuing education"—a manifestation of leisure and affluence—rapidly developing. People are increasingly exposed to the values of the educational and scientific faction and released into the work force of the nation, carrying with them the open-ended perceptions of science, an event which produces a political skepticism and renders them less susceptible to the propaganda of the system. Scientific philosophy becomes more than the foundation of technology. That which demands the open-ended view in its inherent methodology, which is historically epitomized by theoretical and paradigm controversy, currently expressed in the conflict between particle theory, wave theory, and complementarity,[5] between the uncertainty of indeterminacy and the certainty of determinacy, imposes attitudes of receptivity and wonder which find eventual effect in economic, social, and political perception. Such attitudes are increasingly the basis of a civilization wherein educated and organized intelligence is an absolute necessity for survival of the person. The inner demands of modern existence gradually produce an aggregate enlightenment of the population.

"And as for the world in general, all that was or is or ever will be wrong with that is my—our thinking about it."[6] Thus does Lincoln Steffens end his great work on politics and power. Beyond considerations of a factional balance in the technological order looms the educated intelligence of its people, and the important matter of what the nature of that intelligence is. A plenitude of evidence escapes the notice of a frightened liberalism too preoccupied with its "crisis" to make sense of what permeates its present existence, evidence most manifest in the young because they are the products of a scientific civilization who therefore comprehend its dimensions better than others, and are more at home with its realities than those older and committed to traditional modes of thought and perception. But, as noted, others follow. Steffens has hold of the central clue, perceiving science as a universal force moving the world in new directions—moving the liberal order beyond liberalism. The essential power to countervail will remain the liberal configuration of a diversity of factions. And in a world of enormous complexity and jurisdictional magnitude, this may be the best man can do. But the inner requirements of modern civilization enhance the possibilities of balance through the restraining force of a population necessarily educated to the scientific perspective.

9. The Prospects for a Liberal Politics

Some liberals now perceive that the problem of the order does not lie in the "masses" that technology has released, but in the technological condition itself; in a universe of the absurd where reason is lost, where a mechanistic mentality controls events according to a logic—or logical void—of its own, where man is shaped to secret purposes of organization which frustrate his efforts to influence, or even comprehend. The conceptual division between man as subject and nature as object which underlies the material achievement of the West suddenly yields a liberal fear that an autonomous technology will eradicate man, absorbing him through a denial of his utility and, finally, his being. Modern technology derives from the liberal idea. But now liberals propound it as doubtful whether liberal man can control the monster of his own creation, a monster that, in the insatiability of its demands on resources and people, intrudes upon the substance of all actions and thought. Technology is increasingly viewed as possessing a life and will of its own, and that which might countervail appears beyond possibility as the balance dissolves under the force of its impersonal and technical assault. No reason controls events. None are to blame. There is only the working of an overwhelming force that possesses no regard for nature or man.

In the face of an enfeebled liberalism, a conservative malaise takes hold. That which the liberal idea inspires and sets loose, the formation of imperial America, continues, centrally abetted by its gigantic material production which, in fundamental contradiction, the order cannot absorb. The corporate system with its material and imperial necessities, ravages not only nature; it ravages the inner man, feeding on a growing alienation between means and ends. It ravages

113

the balance, making a mockery of the insistence that power is constrained by constitutional imperatives and factional arrangements, spawning the shell of a liberal order, where there is no constitution and there are no arrangements. A vertical integration in production, not only of resources and their employment, but of man as an element of that production, spawns a system of power beyond limits, a system that fills the void guaranteed by the historic failure of countervailing power.

Until now, an apparent harmony prevailed between the liberal conceptions of man and technology, between the classically denied power of the business aristocracy and the market conception of productive innovation. Now the harmony collapses. Discord and conflict emerge. Perceptions sharpen and what appears suddenly in jeopardy are the root ideas of individuality and rights. The more technology strengthens corporate suzerainty over behavior and minds, the less real do these ideas become; the more does the person appear as a pawn in a game of bureaucratic power beyond his comprehension and control; the more do rights resemble an illusory artifact of corporate merchandising. Suspicion grows that the great liberal guarantee of rights, the division of the social universe into the realms of the political, the economic, and the personal, is now evaporated into a bureaucratic leviathan—a suspicion which renders rational the confusing spectacle of a liberal people in angry reaction against the institutions of their own order.

"The salvation of man will not come until skepticism sends out its circuit riders."[1] But now the circuit riders are out, sent by the imperatives of the technological system. In its demand for a population ultimately educated to the attitudes and values of science, the forces of technology transform a skepticism, which resides deep within the methodology of the scientific approach, into a social force, and into a political faction of significant and countervailing effect.

Still, the crisis of liberalism is a crisis of perception. Liberals fail to perceive the scientific realities of the modern age, not because their tradition makes them myopic, but because they have lost contact with the assumptions of that tradition, which visualize power and authority as the political expression of crucial economic position. The modern liberal finally finds liberalism too "Marxist."

He denies it, and so denies the roots of his own history. But those who speak for the "liberal" position are not men of science, at least not consciously. Most identify with philosophy and the arts and, as C. P. Snow makes plain, their ignorance of scientific endeavor is abysmal.[2] Incredibly, they share the prejudice of the technical mind that no important connection exists between science and social speculation. They would not grasp the dilemma of a young Oppenheimer anguishing over whether to become a physicist or a poet, if they took notice of such an event at all. Anxious to accord science to technology, perceiving its emergence, in dread, as the eradication of individuality in human beings, the liberal establishment fails to comprehend the substance of the major political force of its time. The result is a profound inability to grasp the movement of power, an inability which suggests that an ideology out of touch with the economic realities of its own system can no longer influence it.

But more than the economic foundations of liberal thought eludes those who now articulate its principles. In its manifest political expression, Newtonian social philosophy seeks balance through a search for restraining power which exists outside the parameters of power already expressed. Power in motion, representing a countervailing capability, is assumed to be distinct from power in motion already articulated. The universe of Newton is closed, and it is within a given field of forces that balance must take place. Yet, as Einstein and others who speculate about an exploding universe imply, power that can restrain power is inherently a part of the power it checks, because all power is a part of itself.

The unity of opposites; the idea that contradiction exists within the development of events, that the clash of opposing forces, which is the realization of contradiction, results in a higher condition which reflects a more perfect approximation of perfect harmony, is an idea attributed to Hegel, who, indeed, articulates it for the world—or at least for his interpreters. Yet Hegel does not invent the dialectic. Found in less systematic form in earlier Western philosophy since Socrates and before, it patently saturates the liberal tradition. Those who insist that Hegel, and even Marx, are liberals are not fully wrong, and self-defining liberals who reflexively reject their cosmological position demonstrate that within the realm of ideology, as elsewhere, there is no war like a civil war.

The concept of contradiction and dialectical motion is inherent in the liberal idea of man; dual in his nature, striving for a greater balance that will reconcile the clash of opposites—reason and emotion—within; producing the inner tension which dominates the assumptions of liberal man. It is from contradiction that the Newtonian idea of politics commences. While the general contention of Rationalism is that society must imitate nature because the natural is the reasonable, for the liberal Rationalists social reason is a reason of balanced tension, a necessary consequence of the inner conflict of human beings and, by extrapolation, of the political universe.

Hence the real source of contending power is contradiction, and the search for balance must turn inward to the system, where potential opposition is inherent in the events of its development, as the political universe explodes, dialectical in motion, form, and content. In its quest for the balance of Newton, liberalism is led to the logic of Hegel; to an understanding that its traditional commitment to the conception enunciated by Aristotle, that an event cannot be itself and its own opposite at the same instant in time, is simply not useful in social analysis, because it bifurcates what is really one. As the crucial restraint on the emotions within man is the reason also within him—that which allows the historic attempt to comprehend the laws of nature and translate them into a political application—so the potential restraint on corporate power is found within the fundamental realities of that power itself.

It is the contention of Simmel that the creation of form is the central expression of life, and the tendency of established form is to perpetuate itself by resisting the continuing force of life which works to destroy its past manifestations to allow new expression of its creative urge. The struggle between life and form characterizes human existence. Thus the corporate order comes under increasing assault by the liberal idea which creates it. But beyond this, the major intellectual form of Western civilization, the core of the liberal idea for the past four centuries, the Newtonian conception of a universal symmetry and order, is now engaged in struggle with the forces of life greater than itself. This modern struggle is immense in scale, those involved seldom grasping its dimensional totality. In such times, a paradigm shift is in process.

What is initially under attack is the form of the market, on all the fronts so graphically depicted by Wills; the markets of the moral, the economic, the intellectual, and the political;[3] an assault on the essential commitment to man as possessor and specialized producer, on the alienation of human beings from their labor and from themselves, all that the commodity philosophy insists upon as necessary conditions of existence. These become the early targets of a liberalism turned against itself. But its eventual thrust must be against the arrangements of power that are historically retained as the partial reality of the market is transformed into the overwhelming reality of the corporate order. Limited by liberal conceptions, the central proposition of the struggle between life and form becomes a search for the restraint on power that is the supposed result of the overarching idea of constitutionality; a search, more human than liberal, that increasingly discovers its articulation in the emergence of scientific power.

The conflict between life and form thus finds major expression in the perennial quest for balance. But every age imposes its particularities on existence, and the conditions of the twentieth century mold the details of this quest into certain shapes and configurations. Largely unrecognized, it is these which determine the fundamental tensions permeating the contemporary politics of all affluent liberal nations.

Shaped by the facts of technology, the struggle between life and form within an affluent liberalism is expressed in a crucial tension between the values of inquiry and the values of control—between the scientific mind and the technological mind. The scientific endeavor finds its inspiration in philosophy and art—the traditional disciplines of search and speculation—not in the ethos of productive efficiency with which it is frequently and wrongly associated. Technology is not concerned with truth, but with organizational control; a control that poses an inherent threat to the continuation of a scientific philosophy which necessitates the anarchy of an open-ended theory of knowledge as a presupposed attitude.

Science is committed to investigation and discovery, technology to application and technique, and the friction between them dominates the politics of the age. What ultimately sets science, not apart from technology, but against technology as a political force, is a division of political interests which come to be increasingly perceived and understood. The material manifestations of technological achievement seem to characterize the corporate system. But the science this achievement is predicated upon is more deeply characteristic. That it is far more common to identify postindustrial civilization with technology than with science does not alter the fact that the foundation of the modern era is scientific. A technological mentality, pressured by its need for bureaucratic control, may eventually crush scientific inquiry and speculation and, in so doing, destroy the basis of its own existence. Yet, whatever the outcome, the major political fact of the modern age is an inherent struggle between basic historical forces—a struggle between the mind of science and the mind of technology—between life and form.

Nothing, of course, guarantees liberal recognition of the new locus of countervailing power, as nothing inherent in the process of history ensures the preservation of anything resembling the liberal idea. But the notion of factional balance is a vital element of the traditional attempt to control power, a political response to the conception of balance that all men seek in every dimension of their existence. Whether it survives or not, the liberal assumption that operative rights are consequent to the proper ordering of power now grows in intensity and scope. Increasingly the language and ideas of liberalism become a global force, suggesting that something in the liberal promise appeals to what may be general in man. What Goldschmidt describes as "the need for positive affect,"[4] a universal predilection of human beings to project their egos onto the world—to make some difference—is a powerful reality. The formulation of the liberal individual—the most universally attractive element of its ideology—accords with this, permeating the assumptions of many who most fervently assert their fundamental opposition to liberal philosophy.

It is the proposal of Jefferson that the proper function of the elite—if truly composed of "natural aristocrats"—is eventually to incorporate all within itself, thereby achieving its own elimination. The similarity of this to the withering away of the state is more than obvious; it is significant. What results is a democratic distribution of political authority, where there are no elites, and where authority is possessed in absolutely equal proportion by all. But Jeffersonian democracy is a rural doctrine, wherein the data necessary to public decision are relatively simple, and wherein people can easily get in touch with them. In a world of concentrated urban populations, great national and international jurisdictions, and the enormous fact of technological interdependence, the nearest approximation to the democratic idea of an equality of authority is an equality of significant factions—a concept long applauded by a liberal pluralism not, as revealed in its approval of operative elites within factions, because pluralism favors equality, but because it promises balance. While the struggle for an equality of authority among individuals may rage within groups, this must be subsumed by the larger liberal order of groups in conflicts of power; of faction counterposed to faction.

This is a proposition implicit in the contention of certain popular writers, many of them "liberal," who search for new arrangements of power. But, perhaps because the idea of contradiction does not sound Lockian enough, perhaps because power itself is disreputable, none formulate it in terms sufficiently clear to establish the ground for a new theoretical foundation—for a liberalism released from the frustrating demands of its outmoded economic commitments. Still, the antithesis to corporate America lurks within the conditions of its further development. Power explodes and seeks expanded channels and forms of articulation.

This becomes expressed in a growing understanding that politics and economics are not divided realms, but are of organic connection, a difficult proposition for a people nurtured on the notion that society is nothing more than an aggregate of particles which comprise what cannot really exist. It is reflected in the civil rights movement and changing attitudes about and perceptions of race relations in the United States, in the emergence of the women's movement, the consumers' movement, the environmental movement, and white-collar and university unions, all of which represent early political articulations of the impact of affluence and the force of science which produces it as an expanding condition of power. It is manifested in an awareness of surplus; in the growing refusal of human beings to exist on the edge of starvation or within a poverty of desperation. The implications of scientific exploration and abundance reach even into the sovereignty of nations, reflecting that, "in point of material welfare, all the civilized peoples have been drawn together by the state of the industrial arts into a single going concern,"[5] suggestive of the possibility of a global order infused with the values and outlook of science itself. Its most immediate symptom is a generation in quiet revolt, a generation composed of the children of corporatism, nourished on the values of a past world, frustrated by their implicit recognition of the realities of the present, and vitally necessary to the continuation of technological innovation and improvement. They are the source of the organized imagination and discovery necessary to modern science, a science that determines the characteristic reality of the modern world.

Freedom implies power, the urge to power characterizing man because the need for positive affect is inherent. It is unlikely that America will resolve the issue of power in any but liberal terms; that if the liberal ethos is burned out of the American consciousness, its eradication will be a matter of centuries. But power takes many forms. While it cannot be suppressed, its expression need not be an alienated existence. It can become coordinated within the personality, an expression of life itself. Long after capitalism becomes an archaic economic memory, the struggle for power will proceed.

The power of science, as the power of affluence and a new generation, is elusive, its organization implicit, its consciousness confused, but its presence and function historically crucial. Within its necessity lurks the inner contradiction of the current arrangements of power. The political substance of the postindustrial world will depend on a liberalism in "crisis" searching out the clues of preservation in the economic realities of the present, instead of within an assumed tradition; a new perception of potential symmetry; the artist's insight into a dialectical balance still little perceived or comprehended.

To the liberal mentality, rational economic man is a tautology, the pursuit of wealth becoming the liberal definition of human reason itself. Thus does liberalism transform the classical idea "that the human essence is activity in pursuit of a conscious, rational purpose"[6] into the notion that rationality maximizes individual situations and utilities and, ultimately, into the view that the only reasonable behavior is the pursuit of economic gain. If Marx could accuse capitalist economics of a historic aggregation of human alienation, the liberal could insist that labor finds connection to its product through the wages it represents, and the independence it allows. If the liberal finds important inspiration in the elitist politics of Aristotle and the idea of the golden mean, he possesses an importantly different version of the nature of political man. Unlike Aristotle and unlike the democrat who follows in one line of his tradition, for whom man finds himself in politics, the liberal insists that personal fulfillment depends upon isolation from the political, an isolation made possible only by the existence of a Newtonian market that will itself countervail against the state.

But the liberal mind must now confront the fact that the market is dissolved, and that the capitalist element of its own thought is in ideological contradiction with that dimension of civil liberties and individual integrity within liberalism which comprises what is most worthy of civilized preservation. The realization develops that the Lockian right to estate finds ultimate purpose in a more fundamental right, that which Brandeis formulates as "the right to be let alone,"[7] that which underlies the entire range of rights that liberalism attributes to the inherent personality of man.

Yet, the stress on individual rights notwithstanding, the Newtonian order always involves competition among organized structures. As America moves into the epoch of modern technology, such organization increasingly revolves around expertise. A system of countervailing bureaucracies or, in terms of the power of specialized knowledge, countervailing technostructures, becomes the prevailing form of the current world, and an effective liberalism must come to grips with the political implications of this condition. It must infiltrate liberal conceptions that great corporations are beyond nations in interests and loyalties, beyond the confining jurisdictions of governments in their arrangements of international finance and productive power. Of this Lenin warns. But it is not the proletariat which becomes the locus of international response. As the liberal mind comes to realize that balance in the modern world is less national than global, an international science becomes more conscious of itself as a faction in politics. It becomes more manifest that the only force that realistically contends with a multinational corporate reality is the force of organized science, the contradiction of corporatism. How well a liberal politics finds alliance with the force of science, how effectively science, as an operative faction, masters the Byzantine configurations of a technological system of power, are considerations that will control the substance of politics in the modern world.

Liberals must recover awareness of a tradition that insists that balance attained must be preserved; that deviation from symmetry is an automatic expression of tyranny; that a harmony no longer assumable demands a new quest for the potentialities of countervailance. What matters most immediately is perception of interest in postindustrial terms; the pursuit of the Newtonian order through an articulated factional politics predicated, not on a pretense that the old factions continue, but on a new vision of technological conditions and a new understanding of contradiction as a political force of ultimate importance. Those who strive to reestablish the golden age must fail, because there is none and never was. The search for a new balance always requires the implicit or conscious understanding that increased abundance, despite dialectical fluctuations, is the continuing history of human beings, that a new level of affluence invariably creates the conditions of a greater equality of power, that those excluded by any order, including a multinational corporate order, must somehow be admitted for a political system to be possible. The immediate challenge to liberal perception is directed to its ability to divest itself of its historic dependence on the notion of economic scarcity. Liberals must come to realize that the politics of opportunity change as the economics of opportunity find concrete translation in work that demands an intelligence educated to the knowledge and methodology of science, in a condition of abundance that will not tolerate the absence of equity long associated with the historical pressure for the enhancement of material production.

Within the liberal ethos there exists a traditional penchant to stress rights at the expense of economic transformation, centrally revealed in its willingness to "intervene" into "distribution" but not into "production." But far deeper than the commitment of liberalism to capitalist economics is its ultimate saturation in a rational elitism—a conception of the superior reason of the few often degenerating into an attitude of superior worth and a gross snobbery—an elitism so controlling within the liberal ethos that even a basic change in power relations will not bring it to a close. Yet liberal elitism is out of phase with a world where the potential for a balance of power is greater in fact, if less in illusion, than ever existed in an age when liberals were consciously satisfied that the rule of right reason was secure.

As democracy argues that "ordinary" human beings can rule, so science assumes that "ordinary" human beings can understand. Thus the realities of modern production insist that an elitist liberalism attach itself to an inherently egalitarian science and, as part of this, to the struggle for economic democracy, if what remains vital within its political content is to be preserved. Vague as its present power may be, science is the only force that can give shape to this struggle, the only force in a postindustrial world containing the organizational promise of balance—the pervasive appeal of the liberal idea. Technologically, the power of science is plain. But it is the political expression of science that will determine whether liberalism can find release from an archaic commitment to capitalism and, to some extent, from a profoundly acculturated elitism.

Either the present discontent will result in a rejection of the values of a capitalism permeated by a conception of narrow economic man in unrequited struggle with scarcity, and in the advancement of a version of humanity in fuller accord with the demand for inner opportunity which attends the potential of abundance, or the force of science will fail, and a system in imperial retreat will follow the Nazi and Fascist predilection to devour the roots of its own continuation. The liberal necessity becomes an ability to discern the political forces released by contradiction and the expanding reality of politics, to move beyond itself towards more democratic arrangements of economic power; or the constitutional expression of its essential balance must evaporate into an increasingly authoritarian condition.

The central manifestation of contradiction is invariably the struggle between qualities of mind, a historic struggle, raging for as long as human history itself. It is this, "once having marched over the margins of animal necessity ... ,"[8] which increasingly preoccupies the concerns and politics of man. The essential liberal idea that policy is dangerous, that private opportunity and public rationality emerge only out of a proper arrangement of power, that the only reasonable policy is balance itself will, until man *qua* man is fully emerged, continue to be of ultimate importance in the ordering of human affairs. In an era when even the perfectable man of the democrat would be frustrated in the political application of his reason by a pervasive removal—in complexity and literal distance—from facts and events, this formulation of policy cannot be lightly discarded, whatever its historic involvements with economic privilege may be. The proper basis of politics is found within the great liberal proposal for the Newtonian balance, articulated in the language and conceptions not only of a constitutional government, but of a constitutional philosophy which requires an equity of contending forces to secure the major principles of the political sovereignty of the people, contract, and rights. And, within corporate America, forces do

Notes

INTRODUCTION

* H. G. Wells, *Experiment in Autobiography; Discoveries and Conclusions of a Very Ordinary Brain (Since 1866)* (New York: Macmillan Co., 1934), p. 168.

CHAPTER 2

1. Louis Hartz, *The Liberal Tradition in America* (New York: Harcourt, Brace and World, 1955), p. 31.

2. John Adams, "Discourses on Davila," in *The Political Writings of John Adams; Representative Selections*, American Heritage Series, ed. Oskar Piest (New York: Liberal Arts Press, no. 8, ed., with an intro., George A. Peek, Jr. (1954), p. 176 and passim.

3. Thus, "unlike the ancient system . . . Newton's theory enabled all the motions in earth and sky to be reduced to the same formulas and connected with the same laws, so that the whole universe seemed to be subject to one unifying system of law. That system convinced men—indeed the whole mechanistic trend of the seventeenth-century scientific movement produced the result—that the mechanical explanations were the things to look for, even in subjects like biology where we now know that purely mechanical explanations are insufficient. Because of the repercussions that Newton's *Principia* had on many aspects of human thought, we must regard the year 1687 as a most important date in the history of civilisation." Herbert Butterfield, "Newton and his Universe," in *A Short History of Science; A Symposium* (Garden City, N.Y.: Doubleday and Co., Anchor Books, 1959), pp. 58–59.

4. Archibald MacLeish, "America Was Promises," in *Collected Poems; 1917–1952* (Boston: Houghton Mifflin Co., 1952), p. 337 and passim.

5. James Madison, "The Federalist," in Alexander Hamilton, John Jay, and James Madison, *The Federalist; A Commentary on the Constitution of the United States; Being a Collection of Essays Written in Support of the Constitution Agreed Upon September 17, 1787, by the Federal Convention*, no. 47, with an intro. by Edward Meade Earle (New York: Modern Library, n.d.), p. 313.

6. Hartz, *Liberal Tradition in America*, p. 85.

CHAPTER 3

1. See Charles Darwin, *On The Origin of Species by Means of Natural Selection; Or The Preservation of Favoured Races in the Struggle for Life*, rev. ed. (New York: D. Appleton and Co., 1868), especially chapter 14, "Recapitulation and Conclusion," pp. 399-425, and in particular pp. 423-25; and Charles Darwin, *The Descent of Man; and Selection in Relation to Sex*, rev. ed. (New York: D. Appleton and Co., 1897), especially chapter 21, "General Summary and Conclusion," pp. 606-19, and in particular the discussion of "the social instincts," pp. 610-12, and pp. 618-19. What is found here actually provides more of a basis for socialism than for classical capitalism.

2. Garry Wills, *Nixon Agonistes; The Crisis of the Self-Made Man* (Boston: Houghton Mifflin Co., 1970), p. 379 and passim.

CHAPTER 4

1. Norman Jacobson, "Science and History as Ideology; New Men in the Academy" (Paper presented at the 1974 meeting of the Western Political Science Association, Denver, Colorado, April 4, 1974–April 6, 1974), p. 9.

2. C. Wright Mills, *White Collar; The American Middle Classes* (New York: Oxford University Press, 1953), pp. 15-23.

3. Hartz, *Liberal Tradition in America*, p. 11.

4. Thorstein Veblen, *The Engineers and the Price System* (New York: Augustus M. Kelley, Bookseller, 1965), chap. 1, "On the Nature and Uses of Sabotage," pp. 21-26.

5. Charles A. Beard and Mary R. Beard, *The Rise of American Civilization*, with decorations by Wilfred Jones, One Volume Edition (New York: Macmillan Co., 1930), especially, "Introduction," pp. vii, xv, chap. 20, "The Triumph of Business Enterprise," book 2, pp. 166-210, chap. 25, "The Gilded Age," book 2, pp. 383-479, chap. 29, "The Quest for Normalcy," book 2, pp. 663-712, and chap. 30, "The Machine Age," book 2, pp. 713-800.

6. Adolf A. Berle, Jr., and Gardiner C. Means, *The Modern Corporation and Private Property* (New York: Macmillan Co., 1933).

7. James Burnham, *The Managerial Revolution* (Bloomington: Indiana University Press, 1962).

8. John Kenneth Galbraith, *American Capitalism; The Concept of Countervailing Power*, rev. ed. (Boston: Houghton Mifflin Co., 1956).

9. John Kenneth Galbraith, *The New Industrial State* (Boston: Houghton Mifflin Co., 1967), p. 71 and passim.

10. See especially, Veblen, *Engineers and the Price System,* chap. 6, "A Memorandum on a Practicable Soviet of Technicians," pp. 138–169.

CHAPTER 5

1. Paul M. Sweezy, "The American Economy and the Threat of War," *Monthly Review,* November 1950, p. 340 and passim.

CHAPTER 6

1. Gaetano Mosca, *The Ruling Class,* ed. and revised, with an intro., by Arthur Livingston, trans. Hannah D. Kahn (New York: McGraw-Hill Book Co., 1939), p. 70 and passim.

2. Sir Ernest Barker, "Reflections on English Political Theory," *Political Studies; The Journal of the Political Studies Association of The United Kingdom,* 1, no. 1 (1953), p. 8 and passim.

3. Aldous Huxley, *Brave New World* (New York and London: Harper and Brothers, 1946); see especially, Franz Kafka, *Selected Short Stories of Franz Kafka,* trans. Willa and Edwin Muir, ed. with an intro. by Phillip Rahv (New York: Modern Library, 1952), especially, "The Metamorphosis," pp. 19–89; "In the Penal Colony," pp. 90–128; "A Hunger Artist," pp. 188–201; "Investigations of a Dog," pp. 202–55; and "The Burrow," pp. 256–304; *The Castle,* trans. Willa and Edwin Muir (New York: Alfred A. Knopf, 1959); and *The Trial,* trans. Willa and Edwin Muir (New York: Alfred A. Knopf, 1960); George Orwell, *Nineteen Eighty-Four* (New York: Harcourt, Brace and Co., 1949); and B. F. Skinner, *Walden Two,* Macmillan Paperbacks Edition (Toronto: Macmillan Co., 1969).

4. C. B. MacPherson, *The Real World of Democracy* (Oxford: Clarendon Press, 1966), p. 41 and passim. This is, apparently, an extrapolation from the concept "instruments of labour," defined in Karl Marx, *Capital; A Critique of Political Economy,* vol. 1, *The Process of Capitalist Production,* ed. Frederick Engels; trans. from the third German edition by Samuel Moore and Edward Aveling (New York: International Publishers, 1972), pp. 179–83.

C.f., "the owners of the material conditions of labour," Karl Marx, *Critique of the Gotha Programme;* with appendices by Karl Marx, Frederick Engels, and V. I. Lenin; revised translation (New York: International Publishers, 1938), p. 3; "the material conditions of production," Ibid., p. 10, as contrasted with "the personal condition of production, viz., labour power," Ibid., p. 11; and *"the means of labour,"* Ibid., p. 5, from the *Statutes of the International,* written by Marx in November 1864, and presumably unknown to MacPherson, who suggests that he develops the conceptual content of the phrase (*The Real World of Democracy*, p. 43 and passim).

5. Galbraith, *American Capitalism*, p. 63 and passim.

6. C. P. Snow, *The Sleep of Reason* (London: Macmillan & Co., 1968), p. 387.

7. Archibald MacLeish, "'National Purpose,'" in *A Continuing Journey* (Boston: Houghton Mifflin Co., 1967), p. 82. The word "comfortable" is printed as "comfotable" and deserves a [*sic*], although the point is minor, as such matters usually are.

8. Louis Harris, *The Anguish of Change* (New York: W. W. Norton and Co., 1973), pp. 227–28.

CHAPTER 7

1. Noam Chomsky, *American Power and the New Mandarins*, Vintage Books (New York: Random House, 1969).

2. Veblen, *Engineers and the Price System*.

3. Lewis Mumford, *The Condition of Man* (New York: Harcourt, Brace and Co., 1944).

4. This may appear an unusual interpretation to some, yet it is necessary to a real comprehension of the bulk of what Marx contends, especially after 1848. For Marx, reality is categorized into three types: these might be labeled the cosmological, the social, and the historical stage, a device through which the same reality is dealt with in progressively narrower focus. Marx also categorizes reality into the orders of primary, secondary, and tertiary, a device through which a theory of causality is established. Realities of the third order are caused by realities of the second order, and are their reflections, which, in turn, are caused by realities of the first order, and are their reflections. Yet all are real, and part of the same phenomena, which, ultimately, comprise one reality. It is only through this conception of orders that Marx can attempt to talk about all reality, which he does, and "reflections," and "reflections of reflections," which he certainly does.

In a schematic sense, the three types of reality are bisected by the three orders of reality, producing nine categories in all. Thus, for instance, within the category of historical stage, one such stage is capitalism, a first-order reality which is comprised of technology, or the means of production, and the capitalist arrangement of technology, or the mode of production. This is causal to the second-order reality of the capitalist arrangement of society, or the bourgeois class structure, and this, in turn is causal to the third-order reality of capitalist ideology, parliamentary democracy or, more accurately, liberalism.

The point here is that contradictions of historical significance take place within orders of reality, not among them. Accordingly, the bourgeois mode of production does not come into contradiction with the bourgeois class structure. Rather the contradictions within the mode of production cause the contradictions within the class structure. The bourgeois class structure does not come into contradiction with bourgeois ideology, but the contradictions within the class structure, caused by the contradictions within the mode of production, come to cause the contradictions within the ideology. These contradictions are conceived of as developing at differing rates of speed within each category of analysis.

Of course, and especially in his earlier works, Marx employs the word "contradiction" both in an ordinary sense and as a theoretical conception, unfortunately confusing what should not be confused if Marx, in his most profound effort, as the formulator of an attempted general-system theory, is to be understood.

5. Robert L. Heilbroner, *The Future as History; The Historic Currents of Our Time and the Direction in which They are Taking America* (New York: Harper and Brothers, 1960), chap. 1, "The Encounter with History," pp. 11–58, and chap. 2, "The Closing in of History," pp. 59–114.

CHAPTER 8

1. Isaac Deutscher, "Marxism in Our Time," in *Marxism in Our Time,* ed. Tamara Deutscher (San Francisco: Ramparts Press, 1971), p. 23.

2. C. Wright Mills, *The Power Elite* (New York: Oxford University Press, 1956), p. 25.

3. John Strachey, *The Coming Struggle for Power* (New York: Covici-Friede Publishers, 1933), p. 11.

4. Deutscher, "Marxism in Our Time," pp. 20–21.

5. Cf. the principle of complementarity which is formulated by Niels Bohr, and which contends that the theory of particle qualities, and the theory of wave qualities, apparently conflicting theories regarding the ultimate nature of matter, are both useful interpretations, not concurrently, but in alternation with one another. Thus, for Bohr, an event can be equally understood as an authentic particle and an authentic wave, although not simultaneously. The effect of this formulation is to propound a theory of uncertainty, or indeterminacy,

arguing that the varying concepts of reality which are advanced in particle theory and wave theory cannot really be known, but insisting that this is irrelevant to their usefulness as theoretical conceptions.

6. Lincoln Steffens, *The Autobiography of Lincoln Steffens*, complete in one volume, illustrated (New York: Harcourt, Brace and Co., 1931), p. 873.

CHAPTER 9

1. Heywood Broun, *New York World*, June 5, 1925, cited in Harvey Goldberg, "Heywood Broun: A Free Man's Faith," in Harvey Goldberg, ed., *American Radicals: Some Problems and Personalities* (New York and London: Modern Reader Paperbacks; Monthly Review Press, 1969), p. 62.

2. C. P. Snow, *The Two Cultures and the Scientific Revolution* (New York: Cambridge University Press, 1959), pp. 15-17.

3. Wills, *Nixon Agonistes*.

4. Walter Goldschmidt, *Man's Way; A Preface to the Understanding of Human Society*, A Holt-Dryden Book (n.p.: Henry Holt and Co., 1959), p. 26 and passim, especially "The Need for Positive Affect," in chap. 1, "The Biological Constant," pp. 26-30.

5. Veblen, *Engineers and the Price System*, p. 53.

6. MacPherson, *The Real World of Democracy*, p. 50.

7. Louis D. Brandeis and Samuel D. Warren, "The Right to Privacy," *Harvard Law Review* 4 (1890): 193.

8. Carl Sandburg, "The People, Yes," in *The Collected Poems of Carl Sandburg* (New York: Harcourt, Brace and Co., 1950), p. 616.

9. Karl Marx and Frederick Engels, *Manifesto of the Communist Party*, authorized English translation, ed. and annotated by Frederick Engels (New York: International Publishers, 1948), p. 31.

Index